MIXED COMPANY

MIXED COMPANY

By JOHN CHARLES *John* ROBERTSON

Essay Index Reprint Series

BOOKS FOR LIBRARIES PRESS
FREEPORT, NEW YORK

First Published 1939
Reprinted 1970

STANDARD BOOK NUMBER:
8369-1533-X

LIBRARY OF CONGRESS CATALOG CARD NUMBER:
77-107735

PRINTED IN THE UNITED STATES OF AMERICA

TO

My Three Teachers of Greek

HUGH INNIS STRANG
MAURICE HUTTON
BASIL LANNEAU GILDERSLEEVE

PREFACE

THESE essays, selected from papers and addresses written for readers or audiences in Ontario during a period of many years, are published in the hope that they may prove to be of interest to many of the reading public, and may have for them some of the refreshing charm of novelty. This hope might seem to be dashed in advance by certain inauspicious lines of Byron:

> *The company is mixed (the phrase I quote is*
> *As much as saying, they 're below your notice).*

But the high importance for world history and for literature of the various persons associated with the topics here discussed would at once put Byron's disdain out of court.

Then, again, there is a possibility that the very titles of the essays may suggest that type of treatise in which some scholar presents the learned results of his research for the scrutiny of erudite specialists. Far from this being the case, these papers are for Everyman's enjoyment and appreciation; and even at their most serious they avoid, it is hoped, all taint of professorial profundity. And if many of them, naturally, reflect a lifelong interest in the mind and point of view of the ancient Greeks, even these do no more than treat, in an unpedantic way, of various matters of perennial interest in which the ancient and the modern world throw light each upon the other.

But it is not abstruse and technical subjects alone that quickly repel the general reader. As an old saying has it: "Easy writing makes hard reading"; and so, in the revision of these papers for publication, every effort has been made to ensure that, if any parts of them are re-read, it shall be for the pleasure or the profit of a second reading rather than because of any obscurity of thought or heaviness of style.

J. C. R.

Toronto, *25th April* 1939.

CONTENTS

MY FRIEND, THE CURATE

You would be charmed, I am sure, with my friend, the curate of All Souls. Our acquaintance goes back many years to our undergraduate days in a Canadian college, where he chose to forfeit his more than excellent chance for the highest honours of his year by indulging in his one dissipation, the reading of English literature and, especially, of English verse. A certain unpractical strain has always marked him, a touch of unworldliness; and to-day he is labouring in the most contentedly unambitious way in a poverty-stricken parish of this great industrial town, doing much good to others, but laying up for himself no treasure—upon earth. As a student at college, literature and history chiefly appealed to him; for mathematics and the meagre natural science of those days he had no love and little aptitude. He was naturally delighted, therefore, when one day in his reading he came upon Cardinal Newman's reply to the common charge that the study of literature deals with mere words, while science has to do with things; nay, argued Newman, the truer opposition would be between thoughts and things. And I remember, too, how he came to my room one night full of a new find of his: Dr John Brown's sketch of Marjorie Fleming, the amazing eight-year-old child in whose conversation and writings Walter Scott took such delight; and with what gusto he read me good bits here and there; and how he sympathized with Pet Marjorie's outburst against the multiplication table: "the most devilish thing is 8 times 8 and 7 times 7; it is what nature itself can't endure." His reading followed no beaten track; he browsed where chance or fancy led him, having no patience with the professorial view that certain monumental works must needs be read by any who would make the acquaintance of our English writers. In those far-distant years the immortal Alice was little known in Canada, and when one day we were given some stanzas of *The Walrus and the Carpenter* to turn into Greek prose (with all the purple patches of Platonic or Aristophanic idiom we could affix like peacock feathers to our own jackdaw phrases) he was the only one of the class whose twinkling eyes betokened recognition.

It is now many years since he first conceived his curious passion for England. His wide reading of prose and verse had filled his mind with pictures of a land whose scenery and whose history alike drew him with irresistible force. Our psycho-physicists of recent days might suggest, perhaps, that some impulse of heredity influenced him, at the insistent call of transmitted cell-life, which, having for generations developed under English influences, now in an alien environment turned again home. But while, like so many Canadians, he is of extremely variegated ancestry, there is, as a matter of fact, no genuinely English blood in his veins. No, it was the call of the spirit, not of cell tissues. In that great glory of

England, her poetry, which, it has been justly said, is equally instinct with moral elevation and with a sense of Nature's felicities, in histories that spread before him the pageant and the panorama of a thousand years, and in romances and novels that depicted for him the very life and thought of so many periods, localities, and grades of society—in these he found something that fascinated him alike by its beauty and its human interest.

It was the English country scenery and country life that most attracted him. True, he is far from being irresponsive to the impressions to be derived from books or pictures of the surpassing beauty and soaring sublimity of the English cathedrals, the grandeur of feudal castles, and the stateliness of lordly halls and manor-houses, the picturesqueness of the old streets of Shrewsbury or of Chester, the romantic beauty of ruined abbey or ivy-mantled tower, the appeal to the imagination made by Westminster Abbey, the majestic vastness of mighty London. He has read and re-read the copy I sent him of Goldwin Smith's delightful essay, *A Trip to England*; but I am quite sure that he has dwelt longest, and with the keenest pleasure, not on the masterly pages in which England is surveyed with the historian's eye, but on those that tell of English country life and country scenery; on such passages as this, for example: "The characteristic beauty of England, the beauty in which she has no rival, is the beauty of a land which combines the highest cultivation with sylvan greenness, of an ancient land and a land of lovely homes. The

B

country is rolling, and from every rising ground the
eye ranges over a landscape of extraordinary richness
and extraordinary finish. Grey church towers, ham-
lets, mansions, homesteads, cottages, showing themselves everywhere, fill the landscape with human
interest. There is many a more picturesque, there is
no lovelier land than old England; and a great body
of essentially English poetry attests at once the
unique character and the potency of the charm.
The sweetest season is spring, when the landscape is
most intensely green, when the May is in bloom in
all the hedges, and the air is full of its fragrance,
when the meadows are full of cowslips, the banks of
primroses and violets, the woods of the wild hyacinth.
Then you feel the joyous spirit that breathes through
certain idyllic passages of Shakespeare."

Without sharing all my friend's enthusiasm, I can
easily understand it, having heard him dwell so often
and so feelingly on that of which his heart was full,
while he would betray the source of his infatuation by
the constant interweaving in his conversation of lines
or phrases from the English poets from Chaucer to
Tennyson. Not that he obtruded his enthusiasm
upon even his intimate friends; but when once you
did move him to speech, then, like the dying Falstaff,
he "babbled o' green fields." With kindling eye he
would talk of the Forest of Arden, of the copse-woods
and the lanes, of the tangled hedgerows, little lines of
sportive wood run wild, and all alive with birds; of
the blithe matins of the lark, the cuckoo's wandering
voice, the nightingale's eternal passion and eternal

pain; of woody theatres of stateliest view, of im-
memorial elms, of churchyard yews, and monarch
oaks, those green-robed senators of mighty woods;
of the soft music of village bells or the far-off curfew
sounding over some wide-watered shore; of the
spring-time, when daisies pied and violets blue and
lady's-smocks all silver-white and cuckoo-buds of yel-
low hue do paint the meadows with delight; of fields
of dancing daffodils; or of that delightful season when
the broom along the copses runs in veins of gold; of
waters rolling from their mountain springs with a soft,
inland murmur, or of the quiet beauty of lakes and
river-vales, round which meek loveliness is spread, a
softness still and holy. With what manifest enjoyment
he would repeat Browning's "Oh, to be in England
now that April's there"; or the lines Shakespeare puts
into old Gaunt's mouth: "This other Eden, demi-
paradise, this precious stone set in the silver sea," and
the rest of that famous passage; while he forgave Mrs
Browning much for her description of England in
Aurora Leigh as "The ground's most gentle dimple-
ment (as if God's finger touched, but did not press,
in making England), such an up and down of verdure,
a ripple of land."

Yet during all these years he has never once visited
England. He has given himself to his parish, and his
slender income would scarcely, with a decade's saving,
enable him to go abroad; and saving there could be
none for so warm-hearted a man in a neighbourhood
so needy. There has been no sign, however, of chill
penury freezing the genial current of the soul. The

single-hearted devotion, the ready sympathy, the
ardent enthusiasm of his early manhood, still remain
with him. At times I have chided him for so completely sacrificing himself to people who were often
impostors, and for the most part critical and ungrate-
ful; or, again, I have sought to condole with him on
his hard lot and his deprivations. But at such times
he has always met me with a whimsical smile and a
ready retort. In fact, he can marshal a whole battalion
of arguments in support of not visiting the land of his
affection; feathering his darts, as is his wont, with tags
of verse from his beloved poets.

He will, for instance, remind me of the marvellous
power of the fancy and the imagination to body forth,
even out of airy nothing, that which can give to the
heart its deepest satisfaction. "Heard melodies are
sweet, but those unheard are sweeter." Note, he
would say, how, in such pictures as Rossetti's *Sea
Spell* or Watts's *Hope*, the listening ear of the player
bends to echoes from some far-off realm of the spirit,
and hears music far surpassing anything audible to the
senses. And, after all, when one finds beauty in the
world about him, does he not himself half create it,
and only half perceive it? Or, again, quoting Long-
fellow's lines on Chaucer: "As I read, I hear the crow-
ing cock, I hear the note of lark and linnet, and from
every page rise odours of ploughed fields or flowery
mead," he would asked me why the poet's art should
not have the same magic power as the song of the
thrush at the corner of Wood Street to raise amid
squalid city slums a vision of trees and mountains, of

green pasture and flowing river. Where, forsooth, could be found more stirring poems on the sea or on the joys of Bacchus, than the songs of Barry Cornwall? And yet, in all his life, he could never muster courage to cross the Channel, and was the most temperate of valetudinarians. Or, still more to the purpose, what writer has given a more exquisite picture of the scenery and atmosphere of the rich vale of Sparta than Walter Pater, who yet never in the flesh visited the land of Greece? And then he will rally me on my inconsistency and lack of faith in that, lover of Plato though I am, I yet fail to see that the visions of the spirit are fairer and more satisfying far than any perceived by the sensual eye.

Or, taking another line, he will point out the advantage he possesses over any actual visitor to England in being free from all limitations of space and time. No unseasonable weather can hamper his movements or circumscribe his enjoyment. Does he wish to pass from London to the Lakes, or from York to Devon, he can in a moment travel thither. The seasons change as he desires, nor has any Lapland witch such power over the moon as he. "The sunrise wakes the lark to sing, the moonrise wakes the nightingale," but he can listen to their song at any hour of the day; a great comfort, he adds, to such a slug-a-bed as he, who must be so careful about exposure to morning or evening dews. All periods, too, are present to the mind's eye; nothing that he may long to see has passed away from the England of his vision. The inns and stage-coaches of the days of Dickens, the spreading sails of Nelson's line-of-battle ships, the medieval castles thronged with knights returned from Chevy Chase, from Agincourt, or the Crusades, pilgrims such as Chaucer saw wending their way to Canterbury, or Roman legionaries along the Wall, the train-bands of old London, the Devon of Drake and Grenville, the mid-England of George Eliot, Miss Mitford's Village and Cranford, the Bow Bells of Dick Whittington, or the Fleet Street that knew Dr Johnson—all are his to see at any moment. Moreover, he has no need to weep over daffodils that haste away so soon, or to lament bare, ruined choirs, where late the sweet birds sang. Rather to the England of his fancy he might say: "While every fair from fair sometimes declines, yet thy eternal summer shall not fade"; unless, indeed, he choose to have it so, and then in a moment, presto, the summer turns back into the joyous spring-time. Browning complains: "Never the time and the place and the loved one all together"; but he has absolute power to make such combinations as he will, in defiance of space and time or the dull preciseness of unimaginative science. Your dry-as-dust commentator has been known to remark on the impossibility of finding in simultaneous bloom the flowers that Milton would strew on the laureate hearse of Lycidas, or those which decked Eve's nuptial bower, and to doubt whether Shakespeare could really "know a bank where the wild thyme blows, where oxlips and the nodding violet grows, quite over-canopied with luscious woodbine, with sweet musk-roses and with

eglantine." Such people, in his eyes, are but blind
leaders of the blind, and in proof thereof he will quote
me from Keats the poem on *The Realm of Fancy*, which,
he avers, makes with *L'Allegro* a better guide-book to
England than a score of Baedekers or Murrays.

At yet other times he will speak of the disenchant-
ment that so often awaits eager expectation, of the
violent contrast between aspiration and realization,
quoting Shakespeare's words: "All things that are,
are with more pleasure chased than enjoyed." No
doubt, he would confess, his England is largely that
of the poets, who have shed upon it the light that
never was on sea or land. If so, would not actual
vision compel the cry: "Whither is fled the visionary
gleam? Where is it now, the glory and the dream?"
If waking means disillusionment, who would care to
wake to reality from dreams so sweet, dreams that
give zest to life, and that do not in the least interfere
with doing noble things? He told me on one
occasion that he dreaded Wordsworth's experience
on visiting Yarrow: "And is this Yarrow? This the
stream of which my fancy cherished, so faithfully, a
waking dream, an image that hath perished?" They
make no mistake, he held, who remain on safer ground
with Wordsworth in his earlier poem: "We have a
vision of our own; ah! why should we undo it? . . .
Enough if in our hearts we know there 's such a place
as Yarrow."

Then he has often reminded me how a visitor cannot but be distracted by the exigencies of travel and
harassed by the annoyances of the road or of the inn;

petty, doubtless, but sufficient to banish the frame of mind in which one would fain see England. How could one enjoy the most beautiful scenery if he were worried about catching his train or losing his luggage, or if he were in discomfort because of cheerless lodgings or improper food or uncongenial travelling companions? The poet who writes immortal verse on some scene of beauty or of grandeur, can do so only when he is in the proper mood, when everything has conspired to present that of which he writes in its noblest or most alluring aspect, and simultaneously so to prepare the poet's mind that he may add the consecration and the gleam. But the traveller, willy-nilly, must view that bit of scenery just when it happens to come in his itinerary, perhaps in quite different circumstances of sunshine or of moonlight or of weather, quite possibly at the wrong season of the year, and almost certainly in more or less bodily discomfort and mental perturbation, and without the needful preparation of the spirit.

One day I found him in his tiny back garden, gazing mournfully at the meagre results of his labour. "I am going to give up gardening altogether," he said. "The shock of disappointment is too great. When I look at the descriptions and the pictures of flowers and vegetables in the seedsman's catalogue my soul is set on fire, and I wish my garden were a hundred times as large. But see what comes up. No wonder that a garden is associated with the fall of man, the corruption of human nature, and the début of the devil. Your Plato must be right when he

holds that the seal of failure and distortion is set upon
all attempts to realize thought in action, and that
whatever is material fights stubbornly against perfection. Now, if I only let the garden go, I am sure
that I can get undiluted satisfaction from the mere
catalogues, with their alluring pictures of symmetrical
tomatoes and luxuriant clusters of early peas, their
inspiring descriptions of the rainbow-colouring of
irises, and the exquisite richness of tulip or of rose.
There, my friend, I have another ground for resembling England to a garden. I must keep away from
each of them in order to enjoy it to the full, and must
comfort myself as Keats consoled the ineffectual lover
on the Grecian urn: "Yet do not grieve; she cannot
fade, though thou hast not thy bliss; forever shalt
thou love and she be fair."

In all these arguments against visiting England
there has been no discoverable trace of sour grapes.
If there has been disappointment, he gives no sign;
and if on a Sunday he speaks to his flock of compensation, of cheerful resignation, and of faithful attention to the duty next them, that teaching he certainly
has first followed himself. Only once in all these
years have I heard him express anything at all resembling discontent or a wish that things might be otherwise, and then it was no more than the mock-
disconsolate declaiming of Gammer Gurton's lines:

> O that I was where I would be!
>   Then would I be where I am not;
> But where I am I still must be,
>   And where I would be I cannot.

THE ATHENIANS AND SOCRATES

THE whole world has long regarded the condemnation and death of Socrates as a martyrdom not unworthy to be mentioned in the same breath with the tragedy of Calvary, and as an act of gross injustice involving in the deepest disgrace the Athenian people responsible for it. In Plato's deeply moving account in the *Phaedo* of the last hours of Socrates, the concluding words of the narrative pronounce a brief eulogy upon him, couched in language so restrained as to seem at first to be most inadequate and unimpressive. Greek writers, however, preferred that the final scene of a drama, or the close of some great oration, should be on a quiet and subdued note, quite unlike the thrilling effects so dear to our modern histrionic taste. "Such," writes Plato, "was the death of our friend, a man of whom we may say that, of all those of his time that we have known, he was the best and withal the wisest and the most just." Notice the final word, placed with apparent deliberation at the very close, as if to leave in the memory a challenge to the Athenian verdict, a charge of injustice on the part of those who had sworn to dispense justice, and thus, in effect, an appeal to the judgment of posterity. A few years ago the proposal was actually made in Greece that an Athenian court should retry the case, in order that the verdict of 399 B.C. might be formally reversed. It was urged that the Athenian people owed it to themselves thus to put on record their solemn confession that a grave miscarriage of justice had been made by their ancestors of two thousand three hundred years ago. Of course, nothing came of the suggestion. It was doubtless recognized that the judgment had long ago been reversed by a tribunal far more authoritative and august than any court of justice that Greece could convene—by the universal voice of the civilized world and the conscience of mankind.

And yet, without any thought of contesting or deprecating this reversal of judgment by later ages, one may be permitted to raise the question how such a mistake ever came to be made. To suppose that the Athenians were an intolerant and bigoted community, or that they were an unintelligent populace, incapable of discernment, runs counter to the world's settled beliefs about that famous people. A great body of evidence testifies to the intellectual alertness and acumen of the Athenians. It was on this evidence that Sir Francis Galton, the greatest of English anthropologists, based his remarkable estimate that, in mental capacity, the Athenian citizen surpassed the average Englishman as much as the latter does the African native. As for the other explanation, that of intolerance and bigotry, Greece and, in particular, Athens may with entire justice claim to be called the original home of spiritual freedom. For it is not merely for freedom from political domination by the Orient that our modern Western world stands indebted to the Greeks. What we owe to them is much more than the memory and inspiration of Marathon and Salamis, the first and, in many ways, the finest of all recorded battles for human freedom. It was in Greece that the spirit of man first found liberty to expand according to the impulses of its own nature; in Greece, men first set themselves freely to explore every avenue of human development, and to discuss every subject that mankind finds of interest. Freedom of speech and freedom of thought first flourished among the Greeks, and there have been few periods between the loss of Greek independence and the last two centuries when in any country they could be said to exist as unfettered as in the lifetime of Socrates and Plato.

The Greeks had one advantage which not all ages or all countries have enjoyed, that of being free from interference by priestly castes of organized religion. There was nothing resembling the conflict European history has since too often known between the dogmas of the Church and free speculation and inquiry. There were temples and priests in every city, but nowhere any priestly organization or hierarchy whose powerful influence could possibly result in the stifling of discussion and criticism. More than that, there were no creeds in ancient Greece; no theological systems of belief; no articles of religion or catechism whose doctrines people must accept, whether on pain of eternal damnation or merely of social disapproval. No charge of heterodoxy could be laid where no such thing as orthodoxy existed.

Nor, again, was religion in Greece closely and consciously associated with morality. It is told of Lord Melbourne that he was once highly indignant on hearing a sermon which condemned certain immoral practices. "Things," said he, "have come to a pretty pass when religion is allowed to invade the sphere of private life." The noble peer's conception of religion was evidently akin to that of the benighted Southern negro, who at a revival service volubly acknowledged the many sins he had committed in recent years, and then added: "But, thank the Lord, through it all I never lost my religion." The point of these stories would have escaped the ancient Greek, who never thought of religion as the primary source or the chief sanction of moral conduct, or of morality as the finest flower and test of religion.

Greek religion was one of cult rather than of either creed or conduct; it was concerned with rites and observances, not with doctrines and beliefs. The Zeus of one city or temple was not the Zeus of another city or temple, nor was the myth associated with the Apollo of Delos that which was told of the Apollo of Delphi. All manner of liberties might be taken with the numberless legends (often themselves contradictory and irreconcilable) relating to the various gods worshipped throughout Greece. We see this quite clearly in the way in which the tragedians felt free to mould and alter a myth to suit their purpose; nor was the new turn or the fresh interpretation always such as would win greater respect for the particular god concerned. In comedy we may see something stranger

still, when some god is made a ludicrous, or even a
contemptible, figure on the stage, and is represented,
not merely as made in the image of man, but as resembling the most despicable of mankind, a glutton,
a poltroon, a boastful liar, a debauchee, a fool.

In Athens, one might with equal impunity express
belief or disbelief in the accounts given of Athena,
the city's patron deity. Even the avowal of disbelief in the very existence of the gods was scarcely
a punishable offence. The charge of impiety was
reserved rather for those who, by some "overt act
of sacrilege or blasphemy affecting the worship and
ceremonies of the State religion.—(Burnet.)" brought
the city into peril of the divine displeasure. Such an
offence was not regarded as heresy; it was rather a
form of sedition. It was objectionable, and might
be actionable, not because it revealed a deplorably
irreligious mind, but because it seemed to involve
disloyalty to the State and treason to the established
order. In the few cases on record where men were
thus charged with impiety, there always appears this
political aspect of concern for the State religion conceived as something safeguarding the city and ensuring its prosperity. And usually it is easy to see
that the accusers who professed this concern were
not moved by the indignation either of a religious
zealot or of an ardent patriot, but were working to
achieve more personal and private ends. To compass these it was their aim to induce the people to
believe that the accused person was somehow en-
dangering the security and well-being of the com-

munity by his attitude to the established rites of worship.   It is noticeable also that in practically all cases
the charge of impiety is combined with another charge
which, we may suspect, covers a more genuine ground
of offence.*   We are, therefore, far from being justified in assuming that, because so righteous a man
as Socrates was condemned to death for impiety, the
Athenians must have been intolerant and bigoted in
matters of religion.   Nor should we see in his trial
and condemnation a close parallel to the burnings at
the stake which have left so deep a stain upon certain
pages of the history of Christianity.   These latter
were, as a rule, the result of a genuine, though mistaken, zeal for religion; in the Athens of Socrates,
religion was scarcely of sufficient importance to
arouse any comparable zeal or devotion.

How, in fact, could a community be called intolerant
which had tolerated Socrates until he was over seventy
years of age, when (as he himself points out) he would
in the course of nature soon cease to trouble them?
There had been no sudden change of attitude on his
part.   His role of gadfly, however irritating and unwelcome, had not recently been assumed.   For a
generation he had been making himself obnoxious to
various people, some of them influential citizens.
His incessant cross-examinations must have caused
not a little resentment, whether it was some dangerous
illusion that he sought to expose, or hypocritical
pretence, or merely muddle-headed thinking.   These

* In the case of Socrates, he was also charged with "corrupting
the youth" of Athens.

catechizings were usually conducted in public, and although they were often, doubtless, amusing enough to the bystanders, it could not have been a pleasant process to have one's ignorance or inconsistency exposed by the persistent and inescapable, even if perfectly courteous and urbane, cross-questioning of Socrates. This unfailing courtesy itself, too, must have seemed to many to be pure mockery and sarcasm, and there was an added sting in the regular avowal of ignorance on his own part and a deferential desire to learn from others. Someone has pictured Socrates as the sort of man who, if you met him by chance and wished him good-day, would at once pounce upon you with the question: "And just what, sir, might be your definition of a good day?" And, as one Athenian said of him: "When we are drawn into a discussion with Socrates, no matter where we begin, we are always led on by him until we find ourselves giving an account of our way of living, and Socrates never lets us go until he has thoroughly explored us." It was this sort of thing which prompted Macaulay's saying: "The more I read about him, the less I wonder that they poisoned him."

There were cases, again, where his influence over certain youths, however salutary it very likely was, interfered with their fathers' plans for their future careers. Thus colour was given to one of the features of the caricature of Socrates in the *Clouds* of Aristophanes, as a teacher from whom sons learned disrespect for their parents. Above all, Socrates repeatedly gave expression to anti-democratic senti-

ments, and ridiculed the Athenian custom of electing
their magistrates by lot. His view was that only the
man who knows his business can be trusted in any
calling, and only the trained expert in the art of
government should be put in charge of the State's
business. To elect the officers of the State and the
judges by lot or by popular vote is to substitute
ignorance and incapacity for that thorough insight
which alone will produce efficiency. This involved,
of course, the equally undemocratic corollary that
when the true and efficient magistrate has been found,
he should be retained permanently in office. To
judge from the Platonic dialogues, Socrates never
concealed his profound disbelief both in the ability
of the sovereign people to make wise decisions and
in the real understanding of state-craft by their chosen
leaders, even the greatest and best of them.

The question, however, still remains to be answered:
Why, after being allowed to inculcate his views so
freely throughout a long lifetime, was Socrates finally
accused at all of being a baneful influence in Athens,
and why was he accused just when he was? The
political situation in Athens at the turn of the century contains the explanation. The trial of Socrates
occurred shortly after the oligarchic Thirty had been
driven out of power, and democracy had been re-
established in Athens by Thrasybulus and his lieu-
tenant, Anytus, the latter of whom was the leading
accuser of Socrates. The conjunction of events is
significant. The restored democracy set itself in
earnest to the task of reform. It was eager to purge

c

the city of the evil influences that had brought disaster
upon it during the past generation. During all those
years of turmoil, decadence, and defeat, many new
influences had been at work in Athens, bringing into
being a "new learning," an unwonted questioning of
the foundations of belief about government and
morality, a growing irreverence and waywardness
among the younger generation. What was more
natural than to connect the national defeat, the
political and social turmoil, and the decay of parental
authority with the other innovations of the past few
decades, including the new spirit of inquiry fostered
by Socrates and his circle? It is as if one were to
connect (as perhaps some do) the evils of our times
and the very evident deficiencies of modern society
with, let us say, the growth of science, or the extension
of educational opportunities, or the granting of the
franchise to women. So the Athenian democracy felt
that, if ruin had come in the train of these innovations,
then safety for Athens lay in returning to the old ways,
the old standards, and the old beliefs; and we have
here that rare phenomenon in history—a reactionary
movement initiated by radical advocates of reform.
It was to this movement that we owe the tragedy of the
death of Socrates. Nor is this explanation invalidated
by the fact that, apart from his condemnation, the
movement had no considerable or lasting result.
History shows few examples, if any, of progress
achieved by retrogression, and only too many instances
of even the finest projects for civic or national improvement soon "petering out."

With the people in this mood, then, it was not difficult for the enemies of Socrates to persuade a majority
of the court * that his influence had been one of the
evil tendencies that had brought Athens to the verge
of ruin. We may compare the situation in Athens
with what conceivably might have taken place in
Germany immediately after the Great War, if the
masses of the people, sobered by their defeat, had set
about clearing away all the teaching that they felt had
for many years been leading them astray—the doctrine
of might making right, of the State as a superman
above morality, and of the mission of German
militarism to organize the world. Or, better still,
let us try to imagine what might have happened in
the United States if the War had gone against the
allies, and the American people, ruined financially and
humiliated by defeat, had begun to ask whether the
calamity was not due to some of the theories that had
gained currency in recent years, such as Modernism
or Evolution. For one legislature that now pro-
hibits the teaching of evolution in the State schools
and colleges there would be a score; and all prominent

* The vote was apparently 281 to 220. The size of an Athenian
jury made it resemble a mass meeting rather than our conception of
a legal tribunal, with its established procedure, its regard for pre-
cedents, and the presence of a presiding judge trained in the law
and enforcing the rules of evidence. This vote was simply on the
question of guilt. A second vote followed to determine the punishment. Each side was allowed to propose a penalty, and the court had
to choose one or other of these. The accusers demanded death.
Had Socrates proposed exile or some similar alternative, it would
undoubtedly have been accepted. But he declared he should really
be rewarded for his long services to Athens, and finally only yielded
to the urging of his friends sufficiently to propose a fine, but one so
ridiculously small that the second vote was more adverse than the
first.

modernist preachers would be in exile or in prison.
How natural a thing it was for the Athenian democracy to misinterpret the aims of Socrates, and how easy
it was for plausible detractors to misrepresent them,
is suggested by Plato in a humorous comparison of
Socrates to a physician brought to trial by a confec-
tioner before a jury of small boys (*Gorgias*, 521.e).
" 'Boys,' he would say, 'you have suffered many evils
at the hands of this man, who makes your lives
miserable with his lancet and his bitter doses and his
vetoes on what you eat and drink, while I would regale
you with all manner of sweets and dainties.' And if
the physician should say in defence that he had done
all this for the sake of their health, what an outburst of
groans there would be from the youthful jurors."

Nor was the attitude of many who looked askance
at Socrates entirely without some apparent justification. They could (and did) point to certain instances
of the seemingly disastrous results of the teaching of
Socrates. Were not Alcibiades and Critias (the leader
of the Thirty) his associates? And who had done
more than these two men in the recent critical years to
bring sorrow and ruin upon Athens? The ordinary
Athenian citizen could scarcely be expected to realize
that, though these two men had at one time fre-
quented the society of Socrates, he had been unable
to win them to his way of thinking or to leave his
impress on their character; that their depravity
showed, not the extent of his influence over them,
but his failure to influence them.

No one, however, rightly understands the history

of that age who cannot see that, in a certain sense, Socrates *was* a destructive critic and subverter of the established morality, involving, as it did, the subordination of the individual to the community, whereby his character was moulded and his standards of judgment determined.   The fifth century B.C. is one of the great transition periods of the world's history, a period comparable in importance to the era of the Reformation and the Renaissance in Western Europe. At such periods, quite few in number but of incalculable significance in the history of human progress, greater advance may be made in a decade than in an ordinary century or in a cycle of Cathay.   Such periods are times alike of great opportunities and of great perils, when hopes and fears each have their place.   It is not difficult, for instance, to find reasons for believing that the opening of Japan to western civilization has brought greater evils in its train to the Japanese than it has brought blessings.   And one can readily sympathize with those conservative Chinese who were very reluctant to see their countrymen run the risk of moral chaos through losing the old sanctions without any certainty of their being replaced by new.

It was a gain for mankind, undoubtedly, that the change should be made which began in that century in Greece, the change from tradition to reason, from authority to personal conviction, from control by the community to individual independence.   But at the time it was apparently dangerous to the stability of society, and fraught (as are all such ages of momentous change) with danger of moral shipwreck to the individual citizen. At such times it would almost seem as if a generation or two of men were being sacrificed to the progress of humanity. It must needs be that progress should come, but woe unto them through whom it comes. Similarly, to illustrate the nation by the family, there are cases where parents have well-founded reason to regret that they ever sent their sons to college. Not every youth survives unscathed the perilous period of enlightenment and sophistication. For many people it may clearly be far better to remain content with the old anchorage, and not cast off the moorings and launch out on uncharted waters on the chance of reaching a more desirable haven.

In *John Inglesant*, Shorthouse's fine story of life in England and Italy in the days of Milton and Crom-well, we read of the careful education given to Ingle-sant by a sagacious Jesuit priest to fit him for an important mission in life: "He read to him Aris-tophanes, pointing out in him the opposing powers which were at work in the Hellenic life as in the life of every civilized age. He did not conceal from him the amount of right there is in the popular side of plain common sense, nor the soundness of that fear which hesitates to overthrow the popular forms of truth, time-honoured and revered, which, however imperfect they may really be, have become in the eyes of the majority the truth itself." So, too, the pos-sibility that the gratuitous disturbance of genuine, though unenlightened, piety might prove to be grievous disservice was in Tennyson's mind when, in his *In Memoriam*, he addressed one who had worked his way through his doubts about religion to a faith that was, or seemed to be, higher and more rational, and wrote:

> Leave thou thy sister, when she prays,
> Her early Heaven, her happy views;
> Nor thou with shadow'd hint confuse
> A life that leads melodious days.

It is with this same scruple in mind that Plato, in the *Republic*, removes the good old Cephalus, with his upright life and unquestioning faith, from the impending discussion which is going to raise doubts (only to settle them it is true, but still to raise doubts) about the validity of the current belief in morality and uprightness.

When the common man is confronted with those who seem to be turning the world upside down, it takes an immense faith and a much greater knowledge than the ancient Athenian possessed of the history of the growth of the human spirit through the centuries, to be able to exhibit the wisdom and serenity of Gamaliel: "Refrain from these men and let them alone; for if this counsel or this work be of men, it will come to nought; but if it be of God, ye cannot overthrow it." The natural tendency of the conservatively minded and cautious man is to resist all disturbing and upsetting changes and to cry: "Back to the old ways; to go forward is to invite destruction"; and all of us who are no longer young and inexperienced are desirous at times of turning back the hands of the clock, in the implicit belief that "the former days were better than these." We look for the golden age in the past, not in the future, and when faced with unwelcome innovations we resist what the ardent reformer tries in vain to convince us means progress. Sometimes the conservative is wise in his resistance; sometimes he has made grave mistakes. How can one be sure beforehand which it will turn out to be? What irrefutable argument is there, for example, that can prove that the allied powers in the Great War did right in opposing the professed desire of Germany to dominate and organize our western world for our own ultimate good? We did not want our world reorganized and Prussianized, and so we resisted and finally defeated the nation which was going to make all things new. We felt, and we feel, justified in that resistance. But so also many who had voted to condemn Socrates went home feeling justified, fully convinced that they had done a good day's work for the salvation of their country and the welfare of their children. We are inclined to censure the members of the jury as bigoted obscurantists, but many doubtless honestly believed that only in removing the influences that were making for change lay the hope of restoration and peace for Athens. We may call such men short-sighted perhaps; though it is always much easier to be wise long after the event; we may call them, if we will, stupid and narrow-minded; but we can scarcely call them prejudiced, and certainly not maliciously unjust. They were simply, most of them, honest, well-meaning, patriotic, respectable, ordinary folk, just emerging from a shattering defeat in war, and intent on rebuilding the

foundations of their prostrate nation; the sort of
people who, if not perhaps the salt of the earth, are
often lauded by us as the backbone of a community.

Here a brief reference may be made to another
matter that touches the apportionment of blame for
the death of Socrates. In exercising his right to propose an alternative to the demanded penalty of death,
his attitude was such that Socrates has seemed to
many to have quite unnecessarily contributed to the
final verdict by his intransigent and seemingly frivolous
defiance. It is not difficult to find good and sufficient
reasons for the course which he adopted; but for our
present purpose it is enough to point out that if his
uncompromising stand has troubled many sincere
admirers of Socrates, from his own day until now, we
can scarcely wonder at those jurors who had voted
for his acquittal, but were led by his apparent "contempt of court" to change their vote when called on
to cast their second ballot.

Finally, let us return to the view expressed above,
that, in a certain sense, Socrates really was guilty of
subverting Athenian morality. This is not advanced
in any perverse or captious spirit, but as something
profoundly true, whether it is interpreted as being to
the discredit of Socrates, as it was by those who
condemned him, or to his eternal glory, as the world
at large believes. Facing the manifold problems of
his day, Socrates sought to establish moral conduct
on a sounder basis than mere use and wont. He
called on men to think out the problems of life for
themselves, and to be satisfied with nothing short of

a morality which they could justify to their reason. Not that he suggested that the customary code of morals and the traditions handed down from of old were wrong or defective; there is nothing recorded of Socrates like: "Ye have heard that it hath been said . . . But I say unto you." He accepted the time-honoured standards of the community, but he was not content to accept them merely because they had the sanction of age-long custom and public approval. Right is right, he held, because of what it is in itself, by reason of its own essential nature; and to seek to understand what this is, he counted man's highest privilege and his supreme duty. Inevitably, this affects the sovereignty of the State and its claim (hitherto universally, if unconsciously, acknowledged by the Greek mind) to control the moulding of the views and characters of its members. Even if Athens was far from being a "totalitarian" State like Nazi Germany, the State's authority was seriously under-mined by the highly individualistic attitude of Socrates and his refusal to obey the State where he believed it wrong to do so. What the State prescribed in the way of duty and conduct might or might not agree with his own convictions. If they happened to agree, his approval was in no sense due to the sanction or authority of the State; in such a case, if the State was not opposed, neither was it obeyed; it counted for little or nothing in the decision. And if they happened to disagree, then he would obey God rather than man, by which he meant following his own judgment and convictions. But if for each man conscience and reason are to be the ultimate authority, surely this was superseding and undermining the authority of the State, as the Greeks understood it.   It meant bringing about a sweeping revolution and setting men's feet on new, untried, and hitherto unsanctioned paths. Thus, literally and absolutely (to quote Edward Caird), Socrates was guilty of the charges brought against him.   He did corrupt the youth and did bring new gods into Athens, "if it were corrupting the youth to teach them to set reason above authority, and if it were bringing new gods into Athens to appeal to inward conviction as the one authentic voice of God."

SOME GREEK PREJUDICES

SUPPOSE that by means of H. G. Wells's time machine
an intelligent, well-educated man of the present generation were suddenly transported from the England
or America of this year of grace into the midst, one
after another, of the various peoples that have inhabited this globe in past ages, what report would he
bring back? What would be his judgment on what
he had found at different stages of the world's long
history? Ask such a traveller through the ages what
incidents had most interested him, what individuals
had most attracted his regard, and his answer might
not come within a thousand miles or a thousand years
of ancient Greece. But ask him where, as an intelligent, fully developed human being, he had found himself most at home, with what race of people he had
discovered most points of contact and had been able
to enjoy the fullest and most genuine converse—ask
him this, and ancient Greece would have few rivals,
if any, from the dawn of history until, at least, the
Elizabethan age.

Yet this sympathy between Hellenism and the
spirit of our modern times is by no means perfect at
all points. Our standards, our instincts, our ideals,
are far from being wholly those of the Greeks; often,
doubtless, to our profit, but also sometimes to our

loss. Certain of these points of imperfect sympathy are the subject of this essay; certain characteristic attitudes of the Greek mind which, for lack of a better term, are here called prejudices. This word, however, is to be understood as implying neither approval nor disapproval; it is used, as the lawyers say, without prejudice. For, as one man's meat may be another man's poison, so prejudice is a purely relative and subjective term. What seems to one a silly prejudice another may regard as the most obvious good sense. By prejudice, then, nothing is here meant that imputes narrowness of vision, but rather an innate bias or pre-possession that sways the judgment and influences conduct without having been first submitted to the scrutiny and approval of the reason; a predilection rather than a deliberately chosen point of view. Such characteristic Greek prejudices are worth examining, not to pass judgment upon them, and still less to censure them (for they may be as much the intuitions of genius as the aberrations of a warped or undeveloped nature), but in the hope that thereby we may better understand the Greeks, and also, perhaps, ourselves.

Among these instinctive leanings of the Greeks let us first examine in some of its many manifestations their almost universal antipathy to excess and one-sidedness, embodied as it is in one of the oldest and best known of their national sayings: Let naught be in excess (Μηδὲν ἄγαν: literally, nothing too much). Aristotle, in comparing moral virtue to artistic excellence, writes: "This is the reason why we commonly say of successful works that it is impossible to take anything from them or to add anything to them; it is implied that both excess and deficiency are fatal to excellence, while the mean ensures it." This worship of the golden mean is but one aspect of that marvellous sense of form which characterized the Greek, his instinct for symmetry, proportion, measure, and order, of which we find evidences wherever we turn. In almost every one of the great departments or interests of life the genuine Hellenic note is found to be closely associated with this sense of form and this avoidance of extremes. To this factor is due, unmistakably, much of the supreme excellence of Hellenic art and literature. It was, for example, their sense of form that guided the Greeks in the creation and perfection of the various types of literature—types accepted and scarcely added to by succeeding ages. And it was this same sense of form that enabled the Greek gradually to transform the crudeness of archaic art into the noble sculpture that is at once the ideal and the despair of the modern artist. Again, it was this same instinctive craving for order and definiteness of outline that underlay the development of science and philosophy in ancient Greece; for what was the aim of the Greek in these sister movements but to define, to fix and delimit boundaries, to discover and formulate law and order in the seemingly chaotic phenomena both of the world without and of the world within? And, finally, to end these illustrations, in its moral judgments Greece always held moderation, balance, and

harmony essential for ideal living. The typical
Greek virtue is Sophrosyne, moral sanity and poise.

This very virtue of moral poise and sanity, however,
has often been made a matter of reproach to the
Greek. In his insistence on the golden mean and the
avoidance of extremes, he seems to be quite devoid of
that sense of the immeasurable gulf between sin and
righteousness which the Hebrew prophets possessed;
and Aristotle's instructions how best to attain to the
mean in conduct, so as to achieve virtue, suggest much
rather rules of etiquette for polite society than guides
to holy living. "No heart is pure," writes the author
of *Ecce Homo*, "that is not passionate; no virtue is
safe that is not enthusiastic." But the Greek ideal
character seems to be cold and statuesque, as though
Nil admirari were the national motto. Suppress feeling; avoid enthusiasm; so its ethical authorities seem
to preach. Does not Plato warn us against indul-
gence in hearty laughter, and against the display of
sorrow at the loss of even our dearest ones? And
does he not banish from his ideal city every form of
art and poetry that might stimulate the emotions and
fire the heart? Gross sexual immorality he condemns
in the *Republic*, but on what ground? The reason
given is that it betrays vulgarity and want of taste.
Again, Aristotle, in sketching the ideally high-minded
man, the true Greek gentleman, apparently puts on a
level with the highest moral and intellectual qualities
the requirement that he shall speak sedately and walk
with measured and dignified step. "For why should
he be in a hurry," asks Aristotle, "if there are few

things he seriously cares for? And why should his voice be raised to earnestness, if he regards nothing as important?"

There is, admittedly, a striking and significant difference between the Greek standards and our own in this regard, which one should not seek unduly to minimize. But there is also another side to the question, and to understand the Greek attitude aright, due weight must be given to a factor too often forgotten by those who would condemn the Greek for his lack of earnestness and deprecation of enthusiasm in matters of conduct. The Greek, being a true Southerner, was (and still is) by temperament excitable and easily roused to excessive display of feeling. Greek troops, we know, were peculiarly liable to sudden panic; and the keen intelligence of the race was no more rapid in its working than was their susceptibility to passion. Wisely, therefore, the Greek moralists preached restraint; wisely they gave their impressible fellow-countrymen advice the very opposite of that which the more steady and stolid Northerner requires. It is not necessary as a rule to bid an Englishman or a Scotsman to suppress emotion and avoid enthusiasm; he is not given to wearing his heart upon his sleeve; more often he must be urged to throw off his reserve and his apparent indifference and coldness. If the great Greek virtue is Sophrosyne, balance and self-control, that is not because it was a quality which the Greek naturally developed and habitually displayed; it was an acquired, not an innate, excellence, and one attained with great difficulty; and it was given such

prominence by the Greeks, not because it grew up
spontaneously and universally, and might almost be
taken for granted, but because in that quarter they
recognized a sin that easily beset them and that was
hard to overcome. "All virtue," says Aristotle,
"lies in the sphere of the difficult," as Socrates knew
when, on being complimented for having the best
possible temper in the world, he replied that he had
the worst possible temper but the best possible control
of it. Neither in his character nor in the products of
his genius did the Greek sense of form suffice to make
the Greek naturally and without effort harmonious,
statuesque, and self-restrained; but it did enable him
to appreciate the mastery over passions and emotions
that constantly threatened to overpower him, and he
admired self-control as a virtue of supreme value and
attractiveness, but undeniably hard to attain unto.
The great merit of the Greek was not a unique
possession of the virtue of moderation in all things,
but his unique perception of its desirability. Doubtless there were Greeks born with an innate sanity and
self-restraint (Aristides the Just was conceivably such
a one), but they were the exception, just as is the
occasional excitable Hollander or phlegmatic Celt.

Again, we may, I think, legitimately trace to this
condemnation of one-sidedness and excess the Greek
dislike of professionalism, which presents several
aspects deserving notice. Both in the actual education of the Greek communities and in the systems
advocated by theorists like Plato and Aristotle, what

D

was aimed at was the all-round development of all a man's powers so far as these seemed to have a bearing on his efficiency and well-being as a citizen. Specialization and professionalism of the customary modern type were generally and distinctly disapproved. Even Plato, who made division of labour a fundamental principle in his ideal State, and would require of every one, if not quite the fostering of his idiosyncrasies, at least the development of his peculiar aptitudes for serving the common good, yet, in almost the same breath, advocates as his ideal the symmetrical and harmonious development of the whole man. However much he may in certain moods seem to preach an ascetic mortification of the body and the emotions in the interest of the higher life of the intellect and the spirit, he still on the whole shares the normal Hellenic point of view which calls nothing in human nature common or unclean. That every power and faculty, every natural gift is good and is implanted in us to be cultivated and not uprooted, the Greek fully believed; but he also believed that, as in a work of art, every detail must be subordinated to the harmonious perfection of the whole. Whoever it was that coined the saying that one can have too much of a good thing expressed the normal Greek feeling.

The Greek repugnance to anything savouring of professionalism may be illustrated by Aristotle's account of the place of music in education. Undoubtedly too often the mistake is made of assuming that we can find in the pages of Plato and Aristotle an accurate and trustworthy picture of Greek education as it actually was; and one must always be on his guard against arguing from their ideal proposals to the normal Greek practice or point of view. Still, however much these educational reformers may have sought to change the actual state of affairs, their reform or purification proceeded throughout on Hellenic lines. They did not, like Swift in *Gulliver's Travels*, sketch a wholly fanciful picture that by its exaggerated opposition should call attention to existing defects; their aim is rather to set forth what the customary Hellenic practice would be if purged of its impurities and allowed to reveal itself in its true nature.

Of all that Aristotle says about musical education I select for the purpose of illustration this one apparently trivial point: his rejection of the flute as a proper instrument for the education of youth. No doubt the objections of both Plato and Aristotle to the flute reflect a rather widespread dislike and suspicion of that foreign instrument among the Greeks, a feeling shown in the old story of Marsyas and Apollo. The contest between these is rightly believed to symbolize the antagonism between the genuine Greek instrument, the lyre, used regularly in the worship of the national god, Apollo, and the alien Eastern instrument, the flute, which was so closely identified with the orgiastic rites in honour of Cybele, the Great Mother of Asia Minor.

But, leaving aside this national bias, we have an argument urged by Aristotle that shows very clearly the Greek attitude to professionalism. Although he

gives a very much higher place to music as an important element in a liberal education than any educational theorist does to-day, he yet lays down the
principle that no musical instrument should be used
for educational purposes which requires professional
skill to play artistically, none which is so complex or
so difficult that to attain proficiency demands undue
devotion and excessive time. On this ground he
excludes the flute and prefers the easier lyre. Doubtless, also, for a like reason he would object to the piano
as an instrument of cultural education to-day. He
would feel that the amount of time required by most
to master it is out of all proportion to its value, and
that the girl or boy who spends sufficient time to learn
to play the piano even tolerably well must have had
to sacrifice other important elements of a symmetrical
and liberal education. In *Mankind in the Making*
H. G. Wells also condemns the piano in education,
but for a diametrically opposite reason. He argues
that very few learn it sufficiently well to be really good
executants; most are very indifferent and imperfect
players, and, as he puts it, "to have half-learned anything is a lesson in failure." Aristotle would not
object very much, I fancy, to the amateurish per-
formances of most young people on the piano, if
only the ends were attained for which he values
music as a means of education. Mr Wells, on the
contrary, would apparently not object to the great
amount of time consumed if only at the end one should
be skilful enough to rank as a finished performer. The
disapproval and distaste which the modern writer has

for the amateur and dilettante are, in the Greek writer, transferred to the skilled professional. The difference is illuminating.

It is not possible here to do more than glance, in passing, at the term "banausic," applied by the Greeks to those who had not received the all-round, if very amateurish, training of body and mind of the well-born freeman. The word has no equivalent in English, because we do not share the Greek feeling, which would require many pages to make clear in all its aspects. Shakespeare's "base mechanical" comes close to it; and sometimes "narrow and sordid" or "vulgar" will suffice. But if we have no equivalent term of dispraise, we perhaps have the corresponding term of praise in the words "gentlemanly" and "genteel" in some of their worthier uses. The Greek term, which always implies depreciation, if not contempt, was originally used of the worker at a forge, and was then extended to all artisans and manual labourers. Both in body and in mind such people compared unfavourably with those whose position gave them the leisure and the means for the complete and harmonious development at which Greek education aimed. The artisan might have great muscular strength, but he was not apt to have an evenly balanced symmetrical development of the whole physique, and puny and strong alike would be without that graceful bearing which was quite as much the object of the exercises of the Greek gymnasium as physical strength. Even more, the artisan would have lacked both the means and the leisure for that development of mind and character and taste which was the aim of the literary and musical education that the sons of a Greek gentleman received. So at any rate a Greek would think.

When the Son of Sirach in *Ecclesiasticus* contrasts the higher wisdom which "cometh by opportunity of leisure" with the skill of the worker who, although needed to "maintain the fabric of the world," yet never rises above his handicraft, his language is quite in the Greek vein, if not, indeed, directly inspired by contact with Greek writings: "How shall he become wise that holdeth the plow, that driveth oxen and is occupied in their labours, and whose discourse is of the stock of bulls? He will set his heart upon turning his furrows; and his wakefulness is to give his heifers their fodder. So is the smith sitting by the anvil, and considering the unwrought iron; the vapour of the fire will waste his flesh, and in the heat of the furnace will he wrestle with his work; the noise of the hammer will be ever in his ear, and his eyes are upon the pattern of the vessel; he will set his heart upon perfecting his works, and he will be wakeful to adorn them perfectly. So is the potter sitting at his work, and turning the wheel about with his feet, who is always anxiously set at his work, and all his handiwork is by number; he will apply his heart to finish the glazing, and he will be wakeful to make clean the furnace. All these put their trust in their hands; and each becometh wise in his own work." But for all their skill, the writer goes on to declare that, where judgment and counsel are required, these are not the men who are sought out for their wisdom and their spirit of understanding.

When Plato and Aristotle use the word "banausic," however, they are thinking of something deeper than these obvious limitations of the manual labourer. They have in mind the defective outlook of any one who spends his life absorbed in the narrow round of any calling or profession, and who, therefore, having body and mind unsymmetrically developed, falls short of perfect manhood. The Greek language made no distinction between the artisan and the artist, between the sculptor and the stone-mason; and the term "banausic" was as applicable to the architect of the Parthenon as to the meanest cobbler, to the world-famous surgeon or financier as to the navvy or the petty huckster. Moreover, the reproach would attach also to the scientist or the man of letters of to-day who achieves excellence and distinction by exclusive devotion to some branch of knowledge or to some form of literary art, no less than to the pale, undersized, stoop-shouldered factory-hand who toils long hours for scanty wages and who only finds escape from drudgery in drink. So Aristotle pronounces any occupation, art, or study "banausic" if it makes the body or the mind less fit for the full life of the true man and citizen as he conceived it. He includes also all callings followed for wages or salary, as involving loss of leisure and dignity. Furthermore, "there are even some liberal arts, the pursuit of which, *up to a certain point*, is not unworthy of the free citizen, but which, if closely studied with a view to complete mastery, are subject to these same drawbacks."

Among these latter subjects or arts Aristotle would certainly include music, invaluable as he considers it to be in the education of youth for life. In another passage he recommends that the free-born citizen should take up music (both playing and singing), but only when young, and when he is older should be satisfied with being able to appreciate and enjoy good music, while himself refraining from so unbecoming a performance. That this attitude long persisted is shown by some remarks of Plutarch, who, in the introduction to his *Life of Pericles*, tells us that to labour with one's own hands at humble tasks shows that one is indifferent to nobler things. This surprising statement he illustrates by several examples. "No well-bred youth is led by admiration for the statue of Zeus at Olympia or of Hera at Argos to long to be a Phidias or a Polyclitus; nor does delight in their poetry make him wish to be an Anacreon or an Archilochus. For it does not necessarily follow that if the charming grace of the workmanship gives pleasure, the workman himself is worthy of emulation. We may take pleasure in perfumes or dyes; but the dyers and perfumers are vulgar and banausic folk. So when Antisthenes heard that Ismenias was an excellent flute player, he said very properly: 'Well, he's a low sort of fellow; otherwise he would not be so good a player.' And once when Alexander was playing the lyre in a delightfully artistic way, Philip said to him: 'Are you not ashamed to be playing so well?' For (explains Plutarch) it is quite enough if a king can find leisure to listen to others performing." The visiting Shah of Persia was of the same mind, who, on seeing the guests in an English nobleman's house engaged in dancing, wondered why they did not have people hired to do it for them.

Plutarch would never have understood George Herbert's lines: "A servant with this clause Makes drudgery divine; Who sweeps a room as for Thy cause Makes that and the action fine." Nor would Aristotle have had any eulogy for Browning's *Grammarian*, "soul-hydroptic with a sacred thirst." The Greeks would not have been found preaching thoroughness at any cost; the cost, they would think, would usually be too high, and they would be more likely to quote Hesiod's line: "Fools are they who know not how much the half is more than the whole." The belief in symmetry and the golden mean, even at the risk of becoming amateurish and dilettante; the dislike of professional skill, even where specialization would conduce to efficiency—these are thoroughly characteristic of the Greek in all aspects of life. It is said that Herbert Spencer, going one day into the billiard-room of the Athenaeum Club, and finding there only one other member, invited him to a game. Beginning to play with great deliberation, the philosopher missed his first shot. His opponent, after a long run, left off with the balls in a most unfavourable position for Mr Spencer, who promptly made another miss, whereupon the other soon ran out. "Sir," the philosopher said, as he gravely put up his cue, "a certain dexterity in games of skill indicates a well-balanced mind; but expertness such as you have displayed is strong presumptive evidence of an ill-spent youth; I wish you good afternoon." This rebuke the Greek mind would have quite understood. But the Greeks would go further and would condemn Mr Spencer's own way of living. They would think that his own too exclusive devotion to a special field of labour, attended as it was with ill-health and little social intercourse or enjoyment of life, was equally presumptive evidence of an illiberal education and of an ill-spent youth. Our farmers and artisans may envy the leisure of the professor of Greek, and condemn the extravagant salary paid him. He, unhappy man, carries always in his heart the bitter consciousness that the great thinkers whom he so admires would tell him, with the approval of all that noble race, that he has no true leisure, nor has he enjoyed a liberal education; that the life he lives is unworthy of a freeman, and that he himself must be classed with the banausic and the base mechanical.

It was this same specialized professionalism, again, that in time brought about the degradation of Greek athletic sports. The true Hellenic view of gymnastic exercises and games was that they should train and develop the whole bodily constitution, not for the performance of special feats of strength and agility, but in order to secure general serviceableness for the varied needs of the citizen's life, including, of course, in those days fitness for military service. "Sound health, not easily shaken by hardship and accidents of diet, and supporting a vigilant and spirited frame of mind, with adequate bodily activity, seemed a better foundation for life than the power of achieving special muscular feats under highly artificial conditions.—(Bosanquet.)"

But by the end of the fifth century the serpent had entered the garden, with the promise that victories could be more certainly won by a new kind of training and diet. Trainers arose who by scientific treatment aimed, not at the all-round development of healthy bodies, with robust constitutions and graceful carriage, but at more brawny muscles that would be an advantage in some particular type of competition. Special training and a heavier diet would produce great bulk of frame, which was an important factor in boxing and wrestling contests, in which Greek practice did not separate the heavyweight from the lightweight. Or, again, specialized training and exercises could greatly develop the leg muscles for racing, at the expense of the all-round excellence of the whole man. The athlete began to be a professional; his whole life was ordered with a view to victory in his particular specialty, instead of his physical exercise forming but one element in a training for general human well-being. How much better (from the Greek point of view) was the Rugby football of Tom Brown's day, when every boy in the school was in the game, one hundred and fifty to a side, than our modern, scientific contest, fought out by specially trained teams, who often are only not professionals because they are not openly paid for entertaining the

spectators; while their fellow-students are content to
take their exercise in the form of "rooting," and
many more prefer the still less strenuous method of
merely reading in the newspapers about the games
which the few play and the many see and talk about
and bet upon.

And it was not merely men like Socrates, Plato, and
Euripides who condemned the new tendency. They,
like the modern professor who attacks prevailing tendencies in college athletics, might be regarded as
special pleaders for the intellectual life, and, therefore,
naturally unsympathetic to athletic sports. But we
find that in fourth-century Greece, some of the most
distinguished of Greek generals and statesmen echoed
the criticisms of the thinkers. Men like Epaminondas,
Philopoemen, and Alexander, as well as the great
physician, Hippocrates, condemned the athletic training of the day, although they thought highly of the
older, less scientific, kind of bodily exercise. Their
complaint was that the highly specialized, brawny
athlete did not possess the hardy, robust constitution
that could endure the vicissitudes of campaigning.
It has been suggested, with much force, that this
unfitness of the athlete for war goes far to explain the
contempt in which the Romans held Greek sports and
Greek athletics, which they had come to know only
when this professional poison had been working for
several generations. In those days, Greece furnished
athletes innumerable for the amusement of the Roman
world, but was at the same time the very worst
recruiting ground for the army. Athletes were every-

where to be found, but soldiers nowhere. The Greeks had forgotten their motto: "Naught in excess."

Finally, another noteworthy characteristic of the Greek, and of all his prejudices that which was the most persistent, was his deeply rooted instinct for political autonomy, his passionate belief that his city's independence of all external control was necessary for perfect, or even for tolerable, living.   It is one of the commonplaces of Greek histories how this feeling hampered all political development.   Split up into numberless small states by mountain ranges and deep inlets of the sea, Greece never became a united nation. With difficulty, and scarcely even with difficulty, did these warring atoms combine to resist so terrible a menace as the Persian invasion; and every effort to bring about anything like organic union in some group of states was defeated by this ingrained and jealous particularism.

But for this failure there was some compensation. The conditions which fostered this growth of local independence produced also within small compass a wide variety of experience and a multiplicity of types that saved Greece from the dead level of monotonous uniformity so characteristic of the great Eastern civilizations.   The free play of opposite natures, the contact of diverse types of mind, fed that intellectual flame which burned so brightly among the Greeks. Marathon, the prototype of all battles for freedom, not merely saved the West from subjugation to the torpid East, but rendered Europe the further service of enabling Greece to develop along her own lines, and thus to achieve that glorious many-sided civilization which ultimately passed over to the modern world. For this free play of the activities of the human mind, political freedom was at that stage a prerequisite; not merely freedom from foreign domination, but freedom also from their fellow Greeks, from the interferences, the necessary concessions, the mutual accommodations and compromises that must have resulted from the unification of Greek government.

It may seem a paradox that this instinct for independence should co-exist with a ready acceptance of the supremacy of the State over the individual citizen. It was only after Greek political independence was lost and the Macedonian empire set up, that among the philosophers the theory of individual liberty gained a footing. During the time that the Greek cities were autonomous, the philosophers were consistent advocates of the theory that the individual citizen holds to the State the relation that any single organ or member of the body holds to the whole body. As a limb lives only as a member of the whole body, and is useless if sundered, so the individual finds his true life and satisfaction only in playing his part in due subordination to the whole community. Nor was this merely a theory of unpractical visionaries; it was not an idealist's criticism of the existing state of affairs, but a reasoned explanation of the existing state of affairs, and the same belief was shared by the general body of the people. While the Greek states were

jealous of their autonomy, it was exceptional for any
individual citizen to rebel against the authority of the
State, even in spheres of action where we to-day
should never dream of the State's exercising any control. True, Pericles in the *Funeral Speech* contrasts
the freedom which Athens gave her citizens with the
rigid control exercised by Sparta. But it was, nevertheless, quite as true of Athens as of Sparta that
πόλις ἄνδρα διδάσκει, the individual is moulded by
the community; just as this principle, if properly
interpreted, is equally true to-day of "totalitarian"
Germany and the laxest of democracies. For in each
State its customs and institutions and the voice of
public opinion combine to produce the type of character which that particular State values and cherishes.
If an Athenian grew up loving and enjoying a freedom denied to the Spartan, this was not from his own
choice or of his own initiative. It was because that
was the recognized way to develop in the Athenian
the kind of character which the inherited traditions of
Athens approved and fostered. The Athenian character that Pericles praised was not to be got by Spartan
methods of repressive discipline; but Pericles was far
from meaning to say that Athens was not concerned
about the upbringing of her children and the moulding of their character. The father of a family who, in
order to cultivate self-reliance and initiative in his
boys, allows them more liberty than some of his
neighbours do, who are all for rigid discipline and
constant oversight, is not therefore an indifferent
parent. *Laissez faire* may itself be a form of paternal

administration, and Periclean Athens was no Liberty Hall or home of modernistic anarchy.

The explanation of the apparent anomaly may be found in the fact that (as has often been said) the basis of ancient civilization was military rather than industrial. Competition was stronger between communities than between members of the same community. The centripetal tendency prevailed in the latter, the centrifugal in the former. The existence of the State was essential to the well-being of every citizen; deprived of his citizenship in his native community he was everywhere an alien, if not reduced to slavery. The bond of a common interest held the citizen-body together from the instinct of self-preservation. To-day citizenship is not so vitally essential as it then was to a tolerable existence. Not only may the immigrant alien readily acquire a new citizenship, but even without it he may live a life not easily to be distinguished from that of the native-born. Again, there is less danger to-day of the complete disintegration of civilized society than was the case in ancient Greece; we can take for granted much that the ancient world had to fight for; and in this way, too, the bonds tying men to the State have been relaxed. On the other hand, the rise of modern industrialism, and the much greater value set to-day upon wealth (whether as a source of power or as a purveyor of comfort) have made competition between fellow-citizens sometimes as ruthless and unscrupulous as warfare between states was in ancient days. It is not, therefore, so paradoxical, after all, that the Greek world, while obstinately insisting upon individualism in the relations between states, should hold to the theory and practice of paternalism within the State.

But, it may be asked, was not the development of civilization imperilled by the very freedom that fostered it? Do not historians detect just here the fatal flaw that in the end brought ruin upon these pioneers of European civilization? In a word, did not Greece fail because she loved independence not wisely, but too well? Certainly no one believes that in itself it is a good thing for a great nation to cease to be; but there may well be cases where that is the lesser of two evils. The success or failure of a nation should not be estimated solely by its ability to set up and maintain a stable, organized government, any more than a man's life should be counted necessarily a failure because it has come to an early end, or necessarily a success if it has persisted to advanced old age, fortified against all attacks of poverty and pain. The purpose of existence is not merely to exist. The alabaster box must be broken to set free the perfume and the balm; the seed must perish to bring forth more abundantly. So conceivably it may be with a nation; and so apparently it was with Greece. The mission of Greece was in truth incompatible with its persistence as a political entity.

Division of labour and difference of function may exist in world history between those larger groups we call nations, and Greece, it would appear, was called upon to contribute to the upbuilding of humanity in quite a different way from Rome. It was the part of

E

Greece to furnish to European civilization inspiration and the breath of life; Rome was to give the strength of frame that should contain and shelter the living spirit. If that be so, one need have few regrets for the failure of Greece to develop a strong central government such as might have saved her from disintegration and from the dominance of Macedonia and Rome. Under Spartan supremacy, Greece conceivably might have persisted as a nation, but what then would have become of her intellectual and spiritual mission? Such a saving of Greece would have been an untold loss to the world. This does not imply that all the dissensions of Greek states and factions were excusable, or that many grave and needless mistakes are not to be found in their political history. It is not suggested that whatever was, was right. None the less, over against the fact of the political failure of Greece, and particularly of Athens, there must always be set the doubt whether the special gift of the Greek race to humanity could ever have been so inestimably great but for the very spirit of individualism which involved that failure.

This consideration gains force when we reflect that no one thing bequeathed by that ancient people to the world has been so precious a heritage as the spirit of freedom—freedom political, intellectual, and spiritual. In Greece, man first learned to talk frankly, to reason freely, to investigate without let or hindrance, wherever his mortal or immortal welfare is concerned. Neither State nor Church, neither priest nor potentate, had power in Greece to curb or stifle the free activity of

the human reason.   In fact, those other great gifts of
Greece to the world that we commonly enumerate—
her literature, her art, her science, and her philosophy
—these could never have been brought to such brilliance of perfection in any atmosphere but one of
unhampered, yet not unordered, liberty.

It is not necessary for one moment to deny its proper
value to the antithetical principle of authority and
discipline which Rome represents.   The world moves
forward, not in one straight line, nor under the influence of one steadily moving force.   Rather its
progress may be compared to a species of tacking, the
sails spread, now to catch the breeze that blows from
the eternal hills, and now to that which comes from
the unresting sea.   At one epoch in the history of
civilization the momentous thing is to consolidate, to
organize, to build up a strong framework that shall
preserve against disintegration and collapse.   Then
will come a time when there is danger lest the crust
harden too completely, lest the framework intended
to safeguard and to preserve become rather a prison
wall to cabin and confine the spirit; danger, lest
stagnation and the conservatism of age-long tradition
block all progress, and "custom lie upon us with a
weight heavy as frost and deep almost as life."   Then
is the time for the spirit of man to burst the bonds
of authority and custom, and issue forth from what
was fast becoming its prison-house; the time for all
the relaxing forces of nature to liberate and break
up the soil, as in spring-time, for fresh growths and
renewed garnerings.   This alternating process has

unmistakably operated within historical times, and we can readily imagine it at work throughout the prehistoric ages of advancing civilization; but nowhere has the play of the two opposing forces been so clearly seen as in the history of the influence of Greece and Rome.

When one has grasped this principle, and then has reflected how completely the medieval world, both in its secular life and in its theology, was under the dominion of the Roman spirit of subordination to authority, only then does he comprehend why, at the time of the Renaissance, the revived acquaintance with the spirit of Greece (even if at first merely with its pale reflection in Latin literature) should cause such an outburst of activity in all western Europe; why new conceptions should arise of civil and religious liberty; why there should be such a rapid growth of individualism, such a quickened sense of the dignity and high worth of the human reason, such a joyous aspiration for the free development of humanity. In the nineteenth century also, as at the Renaissance, after a somnolent period of subservience to authority, there came again a revival of the Hellenic spirit of reasonable freedom, warring against all obscurantism and repressive authority; the spirit that insists on proving all things and that will hold fast to nothing which the reason disapproves; the spirit which demands the right of unfettered inquiry and investigation, and which, by securing for each individual a larger freedom than had been known before, tends continually to enlarge the opportunities of each to develop fully whatever powers and capacities he may possess. Other influences, to be sure, have combined with the Greek to bring all this about; yet, none the less, we are justified in holding that the spirit which in the last hundred years has moved upon the face of the waters is to be identified with that "eternal spirit of the chainless mind" which first conspicuously stirred the Greek, "the eldest child of liberty."

It is from this point of view that one can most readily grasp the significance of Sir Henry Maine's often-quoted saying: "Except the blind forces of nature, nothing moves in this world that is not Greek in its origin." The same idea has been expressed more temperately by Jebb: "The creative mind of ancient Greece was the greatest originating force which the world has seen." And so, when some moralizer, not infrequently, seeks to enforce his lesson by asking: "And where is Greece to-day?" the same answer may be given to him as to the inquirer in St Paul's for Christopher Wren's monument: "*Circumspice*. Look about you." For Greece, in very truth, is living all about us, wherever there is pure bracing air for our minds and spirits to breathe. Her influence, rightly understood and justly estimated, we cannot escape from if we would; nor would we if we could, for to this western world she spells "the unconquerable mind and freedom's holy flame."

THE SOCIAL IDEALS OF PLATO AND WILLIAM MORRIS

WILLIAM MORRIS, poet, artist, Socialist—this was almost the official title of one of the most charming writers, one of the most interesting characters of the Victorian period. He was a man of singularly varied interests and of manifold gifts, and yet, even in the matter of comprehensiveness and range, to say nothing of weightier matters, far inferior to that noble Greek, at once philosopher, mathematician, prose poet, seer, and reformer, who has so profoundly influenced the thought of succeeding ages. Obviously a short paper can deal only in the most fragmentary way with two such men, even when every other aspect is disregarded than their common interest in the reform of society. What I shall attempt will be to call attention to certain relations between their social ideals as expressed in the *Republic* of Plato and in Morris's *News from Nowhere*, dwelling especially on some significant differences. No attempt will be made to estimate the practical value of their proposals.*

* The *Republic* is not only Plato's unquestioned masterpiece, but the greatest prose writing that has come down to us from ancient Greece; nor is it easy to name any great prose work of modern times that is so sure of immortality. "How many ages have gone by," wrote Emerson, "and he remains unapproached!"

News from Nowhere is called "the most delightful of Utopias" by Ross in his recent (1938) survey of *Utopias Old and New*; and he avows "I would rather have written *News from Nowhere* than almost any other book in the English language."

Because of the greater simplicity of Greek life, especially on its material and industrial side, and its consequent unlikeness to our own life, the details of Plato's proposals are of less importance for our present purpose than a survey of the guiding principles which underlie his conception of the ideal community. Plato himself, also, is chiefly concerned with the establishment of fundamental principles, and, except in a few matters, such as education, gives no detailed or graphic account of the life of the city of his dream, such as we have in *News from Nowhere.*

In Plato's view the perfect life for man is to be found only in a community, and that for two reasons. The capacities of men are limited, so that no one is sufficient to himself; and yet these capacities are so dispersed that what one man lacks, some other can supply. Society, therefore, should be so organized that every one, after receiving an education that both tests and develops his native gifts, may realize to the full all that he is capable of becoming. The perfect State should aim at efficient and harmonious co-operation, where each contributes to the common weal that service for which nature has intended him. There are some few whose best contribution is the ability to govern, the philosopher kings, to whom it has been given to apprehend the eternal principles which are realized in the perfect life of man. To these is assigned a threefold function: (1) the discovery of truth, and the application of ideas to life; (2) the determination of the latent natural powers of each child born into the State; (3) the providing of an education and an environment that shall train and develop to their full capacity the natural endowments of each member of the State.

The reason given by Plato for not going into detail on many points is that, provided sufficiently wise and enlightened rulers can be obtained, they, in their wisdom, will be able to settle all such matters themselves. His chief attention, therefore, is directed to the problem of deciding what kind of selection and of training will provide the State with rulers of the desired ability, and what their mode of life should be. In the course of this discussion, Plato shows himself far in advance of his time in advocating (with certain qualifications) the equality of the sexes; not equality of rights (that is never Plato's point of view), but equality in respect of service. He believed that the civilization of his day did not develop all the capacity that some women possessed, and that these could contribute to the common good much more than their restricted mode of life in Athens permitted. He provides, therefore, that such women as are found capable of it shall receive the same training for leadership in the community as the men.

As for the training received by this governing class (whom Plato calls the guardians, thus combining service with authority), he prescribes a careful discipline and constant testing that will ensure moral stability and loyalty to the cardinal principles of the State, accompanied by a strictly supervised course of literary and musical education that will add to moral strength its needed complement of refinement of taste. Only on such a foundation of character, he holds, can be built that intellectual insight into truth which is the highest and rarest power with which man is endowed. Then, for such of the guardians as have proved capable of attaining this lofty plane, a further elaborate training in science and philosophy is prescribed, followed by many years of full participation in the practical business of administration; and finally, those who, now ripe in years, have endured to the end with complete success become the philosopher kings who are the real rulers and legislators of the State, the other guardians still in training being its executive and administrative officers.

The most striking features in the mode of life prescribed for this guardian class are the half-military, half-monastic simplicity of their daily life and their surroundings; and the strong sense of brotherly unity which leads to their giving up all private possession of property and the enjoyment of family life with wife and children, in order that the ruler may not be tempted to live selfishly for himself, but may devote himself whole-heartedly to the welfare of the community, in which no one should be dearer to him than another. And all through the State, in every class and every relation of life, runs the principle of doing to the best of one's ability that *one* thing which nature has made him most capable of doing. For, on the one hand, the dissipation of energy and attention over many interests means ineffective service, and leads to weakness of character; and, on the other hand, in the realization of his natural capacities lies the truest

happiness of the individual, just as in unselfish co-
operation lies the highest welfare of the community.
Only by wisely guided co-operation can men make the
best of life, and only by doing one thing well can each
one properly co-operate.

In *News from Nowhere*, which Morris calls, "Some
Chapters from a Utopian Romance," we have a vivid
and idyllic sketch of the life of England as it might be
if what he considers the hideous civilization and industrial slavery of the nineteenth century could be
replaced by the life of beauty, fellowship, and joy in
living, in which he believes ideal happiness for mankind would be found. The chief notes of his Utopia
are simplicity and beauty in life; fellowship, equality,
and goodwill among all men, no longer slaves to
commercialism, but finding in their work the artist's
delight and satisfaction; and, as a result, peace and
tranquillity and joy in the hearts of all. Some of the
details of his pictures of the new England of his
vision may help us to realize what these phrases mean.

First, the country itself, and the homes and dress of
the people. London is no longer a desert of brick
and mortar, but has become a cluster of beautiful
villages and towns, whose architecture, whether
unpretentious or richly ornamented, is uniformly
graceful and beautiful. Through it runs the Thames,
a noble and lovely river, of which it is enough to say
that now salmon run high up its pure waters, while
the city is free from fogs and slums, and basks under
a clear sky in the midst of gardens and pleasant fields
and forest glades. All over England the same trans-

formation has taken place. The unsightly manufacturing towns are gone and, while the population remains the same as in the nineteenth century, it is "more spread," so that the country districts are more populous (for the people delight in country life), and the towns, no longer crowded, differ little, except in size, from the villages of the countryside.

The dress of the people, like their homes, is a delight to the eye, and the people themselves are wholesome to look upon, happy and well built; their manner of life has made them both healthier and more comely, so that the woman of forty looks as young and blooming as the maiden of twenty does now. In one chapter we find people working joyously in the hay-fields as if keeping holiday; the women dressed in light woollen garb, gaily embroidered, or even in silk, the men all clad in white flannel embroidered in bright colours, so that the meadow looked like a tulip-bed because of them; all working deliberately, but well and steadily, though as noisy with merry talk as a grove of autumn starlings. And these haymakers not only seem, but really are, holiday-makers, who delight in exercise and in the country life, and have given up their life in town for a few weeks to enjoy the delights of a midsummer hay-field amid the delicious sounds and scents of the pleasant river-side. This one scene has been given in some detail to show how changed is the whole spirit of the new life; and yet, impossible as the scene may be, Morris's genius has made it appear, in its own setting, as natural as the gay plumage and joyous songs of the birds that haunt those sunny meadows.   So far as the landscape and the external appearance of things and people are concerned, those who know their Ruskin can form a fairly accurate picture of the regenerate England of Morris's romance by imagining an England such as Ruskin would have found delight and satisfaction in.

But for our present purpose it is more important to pass to the mode of life and the institutions of the people.   Here, too, there is change at every turn. The people are no longer divided into the two rival classes of employer and employee, or capitalist and labour.   Brotherhood and equality prevail, not competition and inequality.   There is no longer to be found anywhere the eager desire to grasp as much as possible of the fruits of another's labour.   The struggle for life (which, according to Morris, is the struggle for a slave's rations on the one side, and, on the other, for a bouncing share of the slaveholder's privilege) no longer forces men to create artificial needs that they may enrich themselves by satisfying them; no longer leads to cheapening of production, which, Morris holds, usually means making wares to sell and not to use, of inferior quality and workmanship, but bought because they are cheap, that is, produced with the least possible exercise of care and workmanship; no longer leads to attempts to open up new markets, which, in his eyes, merely means creating new wants among helpless, hapless, inferior races, who have to sell themselves into a new slavery of toil in order to be able to purchase the ugly and unnecessary wares of civilization.

The degradation and sordidness of the workman's life is gone. The necessities of life, even of refined life, are, after all, really few and obtainable with comparatively little toil. And so, in this new epoch, men have been able to discard the labour-saving machinery that has so signally failed to lessen labour in the world, and what they need is chiefly made by hand. Thus the maker, possessing leisure, and able to choose the work he likes best to do, is able to do it well and to produce what is artistic and beautiful. He loves his handicraft as the true musician or the true artist loves to exercise his gifts, and he is, therefore, not eager to escape from his work or to invent a machine to do it for him. Beauty, serviceability, and good workmanship are alone considered in production; and joy in creating articles of beauty and use has taken the place of the enforced drudgery of former days.

As men love their work for its own sake and delight in it, and as brotherhood and fellowship everywhere exist, there is no such thing as buying and selling, no coinage, even no bartering. Stores and markets do exist, but only that the surplus products may be brought together to a convenient place for those who wish to come and take freely what they want. These stores are tended either by people who take delight in keeping things in order, or by young people to whom the handling of various objects is a sort of education, and these, too, engage in this employment for a time because they like to, not because they must. (It may be noted here that Plato, while not entirely dispensing with the commercial class of middlemen, has no high opinion of them. In the *Republic* their function is relegated to those who, because of physical infirmity, are capable of no other useful service to the community.)

Private property and the desire for riches having been abolished, it follows that poverty, too, has disappeared. There is held yearly, in what had once been the East End slums of London, a festival called the Clearing of Misery, at which a traditional feature is the singing of Hood's *Song of a Shirt*. But not one of the people who sing this song is aware of its real meaning; its tragedy has grown inconceivable to them. And crime has gone, too; for Morris regards crime as being, not occasional error or transgression, but the habitual actions of people driven into enmity to society. Criminal and civil law are, therefore, virtually abolished, and the divorce courts have vanished, too. In this Utopia, marriage and divorce are matters entirely of personal agreement, in which the sexes are on an absolute equality, and no one dreams of attempting to force love and sentiment to obey civil contracts. Politics and militarism, too, are gone, and government is reduced to a minimum. Men still differ about the advisability of this course or that, but, as Morris puts it, a man no more needs an elaborate system of government, with its army, navy, and police, to force him to give way to the majority of his equals, than he needs a similar machinery to make him understand that his head and a stone wall cannot occupy the same space at the same time. And so government is reduced to something like the New England town meetings, called to talk over what may be desirable in the locality, and to ascertain what the neighbours think of the new proposals.

The people, finally, do not live in common in large barracks or phalansteries, as in some Utopian socialistic communities, but live as they like; and as a rule they like to live with certain housemates whom they have got used to. Separate households are the rule, but houses are freely open to guests who wish to come and fall in with the ways of the household. The only recourse against unpleasant companions is to send them to Coventry, but that is usually effectual.

Such, in brief outline, is the life Morris depicts for us. The story itself (though the plot is slight) is as different from this sketch of the institutions existing in the new epoch as a living human being is from its skeleton. But the outline may serve to illustrate the principles which underlie Morris's ideal of life: joy in living; joy in producing works of beauty and service-ability; fellowship, equality, and goodwill.

In spite of many differences, the student of Plato, on reading for the first time *News from Nowhere*, cannot but be struck by the great similarity of attitude and even of detail. The important correspondences seem to be reducible to three:

(1) The doctrine of co-operation and reciprocity of service, brotherly unity, and mutual goodwill; the belief that the only natural and satisfactory life for man is in community and fellowship with others.

(2) The belief that virtuous activities (Aristotle's phrase, to be sure, for all activities that are excellent after their kind, but none the less Plato's conception) are their own exceeding great reward; that man's happiness and highest well-being consist in the due exercise and realization of his capacities; this thought of Plato's is traceable all through Morris:

" 'How [do] you get people to work when there is no reward of labour, and especially, how [do] you get them to work strenuously?'

" 'No reward of labour?' said Hammond gravely. 'The reward of labour is life. Is that not enough?'

" 'But no reward for especially good work,' quoth I.

" 'Plenty of reward,' said he, 'the reward of creation—the wages which God gets.' "

(3) The conviction that the perfect life for man is possible only when he is in his proper environment and under right institutions. To both Plato and Morris, therefore, the all-important thing is to have a certain organization of society established which will determine the growth and development of all its members and make it difficult for any one to go astray. It is perhaps unnecessary to say that both have not a little of the temper of the doctrinaire, and give small heed to practicable ways of making so vast a change.

But the differences between the two ideals are even more significant than the resemblances and deserve discussion at greater length. In the first place there is nothing whatever said by Morris of those innate

and ineradicable differences between man and man
of which Plato makes so much; nothing of that
necessary division into classes, based on differences
of inborn capabilities and, therefore, of function, on
which the whole structure of the *Republic* is built.

This may in part seem to be accounted for as resulting from the modern repudiation of caste and slavery,
from the greater emphasis now laid on democracy and
the brotherhood of man.   And Morris, elsewhere, in
one of his lectures on Art, while praising the simple,
dignified, almost perfect life of the Athenian citizen,
yet objects that his civilization was founded on slavery;
he points out that, while the ancient peoples showed
us for ever what blessings are found in freedom of
life and thought, yet they kept all these blessings for
a few of themselves.   Indeed, he thinks that it was
just because it was chained to slavery and exclusive-
ness that ancient civilization collapsed.   So Morris
himself insists on equality, making the aspiration
after complete equality the bond of all happy human
society; he insists on the democratization of art, pre-
ferring that art should for a time leave the world
rather than be confined to a few exceptional people;
he insists that there must be no "residuum" or "sub-
merged tenth"; that civilization is merely organized
injustice and a disguised slavery if it does not aim at
giving some share in the happiness and dignity of life
to all the people.   Of course, in Plato's *Republic* also
there is equality, in the sense that every one is to have
the opportunity of making the best of himself; but
Plato cannot but think that Nature herself has settled

F

the question, by making the majority incapable of living the true full life of humanity, which is therefore confined to a comparatively few exceptionally dowered men.

On further reflection, however, we see that this difference is due to something more than the fact that Plato is, in a sense, aristocratic, and Morris democratic; that it is really due to a fundamental divergence between the respective ideals they cherish. Plato measures men by their power of intellectual insight (not as distinct from, but as inseparably linked with, moral goodness and the spiritual vision); and certain forms of human activity, those of the mind and reason, he holds to be intrinsically higher and nobler than others. Yet to this higher life obviously only the gifted few can attain. But Morris's ideal is the happiness that comes from doing *anything* well and artistically, a happiness that may be attained by the dustman and the housemaid as well as by the sculptor and the poet.

If the possession and exercise of certain rare powers be the most desirable thing in life, then obviously men are not equal, and Plato was right in saying that the fault of Athenian democracy was that it regarded as equal what God had made unequal. But if the ideal in life is to be, as Morris has it, an "art made by the people and for the people, a joy to the maker and to the user"; if the great object mankind should strive for is "the Democracy of Art, the ennobling of daily and common work"; and if the greatest blessing we can have is gained, not by the acquisition, after laborious and long-continued discipline and study, of an insight into the meaning of life and of the universe, but by "the present pleasure of ordinary daily life"—then men may easily be looked on as equal in capacity for attaining the ideal and for living the perfect life. For Morris seems to think one faculty about as good as another; and if any special place must be given to the contemplation of truth and the love of knowledge, it is below, rather than above, the mechanical arts and handicrafts.

A second reason for the different attitude of the two writers is to be found in their different personality and in the character of the times in which they lived. All Utopian literature is coloured by the conditions of its birth, and may, therefore, have a biographical and an historical interest as well as a speculative interest. The mere fact that the one writer was an artist, the other a philosopher, explains many of the differences, both in point of view and in emphasis. Again, Morris, while in name and theory a Socialist, was in reality intensely individualistic in his manner of life and thought. A writer in the *Art Journal* says: "To see him was to know him for a rebel born. He was inclined to divide men into two classes, flunkeys and rebels. . . . Conformity to him was slavery. He would follow no custom. Usage? That was a reason for not doing likewise. His behaviour was individualistic. . . . He dressed, spoke, did as he pleased himself, and had nothing but contempt for orthodoxy of whatever kind." He once told his friend, Theodore Watts-Dunton, that civilization was the greatest curse that

had ever fallen on the human race. He was imbued
with the wild free spirit of the Scandinavian sagas,
which were one of his enthusiasms, and from his
appearance he might have been a Norse viking himself, owing allegiance to none. It was said of him
that, if his own views had prevailed and radical
Socialism had been established in England, he would
promptly have become a bitter foe of the reconstituted
society, and would soon have been put to death as
a dangerous enemy to Socialism. So individualistic
was he that he actually declared that governmental or
State Socialism, with its regulation of wages and
prices by law, would simply bring men back to a
condition approaching the Roman doles to the poor.

Plato, on the other hand, was a thorough-going
believer in paternalism. Most men, he thought,
would be infinitely better off if their occupations,
their amusements, their reading, their diet, their
whole life, in short, were determined for them by
the superior wisdom of an enlightened government.
The difference is illustrated by their views of marriage,
where Plato proposed a degree of supervision and
interference which the modern world, for all its talk
about eugenics, would not submit to for a moment.
In truth, it is something like Anarchism rather than
Socialism that we find in *News from Nowhere*. The
almost total absence of any form of government, the
insistence upon freedom, the complete licence to each
man to do exactly what work he pleases and to do it
as he pleases—all this is at the opposite pole from
Plato's regimentation of men's lives and his insistence

on restriction to one occupation, and that, too, one chosen for, rather than by, each man. The England which Morris pictures is, in many respects, in its versatility, its freedom, its eagerness, suggestive of the ideal Athens of Pericles' *Funeral Speech,* while Plato drew not a little of his inspiration from the rigidly disciplined life of Sparta which that speech condemns.

Then, too, there is the difference due to the civilization with which each was familiar. We need never expect to hear the last word from Socialism or Radicalism; as conditions change from age to age, men will insist now on this, now on that, as the one pressing and essential reform. The evils of our times against which Morris inveighs — sordid commercialism, unrighteous and unlimited competition, industrial slavery, the degradation of humanity to the pursuit of wealth, the exploitation of the helpless— these were not in Plato's day the conspicuous evils they have since become. And so Plato, in the few lines he gives to economic abuses, seems to feel that an apology is due for referring at all to matters so sordid and superficial.

Similarly, the entirely different attitude of the two writers to the principle of division of labour proceeds, not from any fundamental opposition, but from the different conditions in which they found themselves. Athenian democracy cannot be fully understood apart from the institution of the lot in the yearly choice of its innumerable magistrates and officials. In theory, every citizen was assumed to be equally competent to fill any of these posts for the yearly term of office, and the fairest and easiest mode of selection, and the most democratic, was by the lot. Pericles was not blind to the evils that might result from so haphazard a system, but he hoped to educate the citizens by enabling them to share in the fullness of a many-sided civic life, and thus to lessen the dangers of inexperience. Plato, coming a generation later in less hopeful times, criticizes the assumption that even the quick-witted Athenian was versatile enough to manage his own affairs, to fight the city's battles, to sit in the assembly and in the law courts, and to fill any office of state in his turn with entire satisfaction. Most men have no more than one talent, and should concentrate on making a success of that. Hence, the principle of division of labour is insisted upon by Plato in all spheres of endeavour, as a safeguard against inefficient versatility and ambitious incompetence.*

But in the modern world, where this principle of division of labour has been very widely adopted, it has been carried to such an extreme as itself to become a source of danger. In the industrial world, the minute division of labour has brought it about that a workman nowadays very seldom makes the whole of anything. The finished article has passed through scores of hands, and, as a result, the workman tends

* Compare John Stuart Mill's remark that Plato's doctrine of philosopher-kings "was an exaggerated protest against the notion that any man is fit for any duty; a phrase which is the extreme formulation of that indifference to special qualifications and to the superiority of one mind over another, to which there is more or less tendency in all popular governments, and doubtless at Athens, as well as in the United States and in Great Britain."

to become simply an "animated machine" (which is Aristotle's definition of a slave), or even the mere attendant upon an inanimate machine, in daily danger of being supplanted by some newly invented improvement in the machine. His work tends to become monotonous and wearisome, and little, or none, of the joy of the creator and artist remains to him. So while Plato the Socialist insists on division of labour as the cardinal principle of his State, and in his eyes versatility is an evil to be avoided, Morris the Socialist takes the opposite view, not because of any fundamental disagreement, but because of the accident of their living in different times. Circumstances have led the one to seek above all things to avoid fickleness and incompetence, and the other to avoid monotony and joylessness.

The third and last point of contrast to be noted is more far-reaching than either of the others. The ideal to which Morris looks forward is essentially materialistic, as opposed to the spiritual aim of Plato (if the word "spiritual" be understood as including also all that belongs to the mind and thought). Human welfare with Morris is very much a matter of physical conditions; beyond the present life he never looks, and in this present life what he dwells on is always the beauty of material things, the delight in physical health and beauty, the joy, not of high thought, but of skilful handiwork. "She led me up close to the house and laid her shapely sun-browned hand and arm on the lichened wall as if to embrace it, and cried out, 'O me, O me! How I love the earth,

and the seasons, and weather, and all things that deal
with it, and all that grows out of it—as this has
done.' " And again: "The spirit of the new day [is]
delight in the life of the world; intense and over-
weening love of the very skin and surface of the earth
on which man dwells. . . . The boundless curiosity
in the ways and thoughts of men which was the mood
of the ancient Greek [is] gone." And still again:
" After all it is the world we live in which interests us.
The phenomena of earth and sky—these are our books
in these days." These words are not exceptional, but
typical. Joyous beauty, radiant health, exuberant
life, the passionate joy of living—this is the highest
aspiration of the dwellers in this new world. In
conformity with this the education of the young is not
designed, as in the *Republic*, to develop character and
to strengthen the powers of the mind, but only to
teach them how to do things with their hands.
Another sign of materialism is the theory that the
whole foundation of society rests on material necessities and economic conditions. Yet the devotion of
Morris to art, and his enthusiasm for beauty, prevent
him from being completely engrossed, as many
Socialist theorists are, with the dull level of utilitarian
comfort or (in Burke's phrase) with "things subservient only to the gross animal existence of a
temporary and perishable nature."

How different all this is from the idealistic spirit of
Plato it is needless to portray; indeed, Plato seems too
often to go quite to the other extreme and unduly to
despise the things of sense. Yet though in theory he

may depreciate the world in which we find ourselves,
every careful reader of Plato is not long in discovering
that he has as keen an eye for the beauty of heaven
and earth as any poet of his day. Is it not, indeed,
the vision of beauty in the world about us that, according to him, first kindles in the soul a longing for the
vision of eternal beauty? Morris goes no further
than the beauty of earth and sky; Plato sees through
and beyond all sensual beauty a spiritual vision of
better things. For Morris, the lust of the eye and
of the flesh seem to suffice; Plato holds with Shelley
that "Life, like a dome of many-coloured glass,
Stains the white radiance of eternity."

A different aspect of Morris's materialism is shown
in the frequency with which in his poetry the note of
joy in life is overshadowed by the certainty of death,
as in these lines from *Jason*:

> Ah! what begetteth all this storm of bliss
> But Death himself, who crying solemnly
> E'en from the heart of sweet Forgetfulness
> Bids us "Rejoice, lest pleasureless ye die.
> Within a little time must ye go by.
> Stretch forth your open hands and while ye live
> Take all the gifts that Death and Life may give."

But in *News from Nowhere* he puts the thought of death
aside, and displays an almost feverish eagerness to
enjoy whatever is beautiful and delightful in life, with
no thought of aught beyond; while in Plato, with his
firm faith in the immortality of the soul, we find
repeatedly the conception of this life being a preparation for another and fuller existence, when the soul

shall be free from the trammels of the body and the limitations imposed by "this muddy vesture of decay."

In two respects, then, the ideal of Morris is material, as compared with Plato's: first, he has no thought of anything beyond this present life; and, secondly, even in this present life he regards the things of the mind as of less value than the delights of the senses. You will not match in Plato the following attempt to translate into the familiar emotions of our ordinary experience the impression produced on the dwellers in his Utopia by the joyous realization of their ideals:

" 'Do you remember anything like that, guest, in the country from which you come?'

" 'Yes, when I was a happy child on a sunny holiday, and had everything that I could think of.' "

Plato, in spite of a partial resemblance between his myth of *Reminiscence* and Wordsworth's *Ode on Immortality*, could never have shared the English poet's view of the child's enviable felicity; nor would any thoughtful Greek regard the happiness of the child as the ideal for a man to aspire after; but it not unfairly may be said to represent the highest felicity of which Morris dreams.

To be sure, there is something very like this attitude among the Greeks. Much of the peculiar Greek spirit consists in the limitation of the ideal of perfection to this present life; as Symonds puts it, "to yearn for more than life affords was reckoned a disease." And if it be true that joy in physical life and the symmetry of physical powers constitute the Greek ideal, then we must recognize something in Plato not typically Greek.

But there is always something more in the Greek point of view than this note which Morris catches. For example, the recurrent Greek word, καλός, so inadequately translated by "beautiful," means much more than we associate with the notion of beauty. The Greeks are often, but wrongly, said to have had a purely aesthetic ideal; rather, they united the aesthetical and the ethical in a way that baffles both our understanding and our language. Nor is it any truer to say that the only conception of good they recognized was what we call beauty and symmetry and harmony. It would be better to say that they held that nothing can be truly beautiful if it be not good also, and nothing can be good and yet not beautiful. To the Greek, that is καλός to which the uncorrupted heart of man goes out with instant acceptance and joyous welcome; that which, without any consideration of profit or pleasure, satisfies the real longings and aspirations of human nature, and needs no other justification for itself than that it does satisfy them. The term is applied not only to material things and outward forms, but equally to thoughts and actions and characters. Finally, "whatsoever things are true, whatsoever things are honourable, whatsoever things are just, whatsoever things are pure, whatsoever things are lovely, whatsoever things are of good report; if there be any virtue, and if there be any praise"—all these things are καλά to the Greeks.

We are also in danger of some error when we talk of the Greek always fashioning his gods and his ideals after human forms and human life. There is a great difference between looking upon the beauty and fullness of mere human life as the highest ideal we can imagine (as Morris seems to do), and viewing one's ideal always after the image of a beautiful and perfect human life (as the best of the Greeks did). The former leads, at best, to a refined materialism; the latter may point towards a vision of the divine incarnated in man. The former looks only at earth, and calls it heaven; the latter seeks to bring heaven into touch with earth.

May it not be said that the peculiar Greek note was a unique combination of spiritual idealism with a keen love of life and of human nature as it is? To-day we are apt to find these disjoined. Where the attitude prevails of contented enjoyment with what this present life affords, the spiritual vision is obscured or lost; but that is Paganism rather than Hellenism. On the other hand, where idealism and the spiritual outlook are found, there is apt to be deep dissatisfaction with human nature as well as a certain suspicion of the world and its activities. The Greek, in some now unattainable way, managed to combine both characteristics, and hence in large measure comes that fusion of unbounded aspiration with contented limitation which so baffles the comprehension of us moderns.

So, in spite of a certain resemblance to Morris's attitude, the ideal of Greece is spiritual, after all. Certainly the ideal of her choicest spirits, and even perhaps the characteristic outlook of her people as a whole, goes beyond the merely physical and material

in life.   And Greece is remembered, and Greece still
sways the thoughts of men, not chiefly because she
was artistic, not because, in the fresh enjoyment of
life and beauty, she rejected Oriental asceticism, still
less because of her political institutions or her material
achievements; but because, amid all the frankly
accepted beauty and glory of her physical and material
existence, she looked not merely at the things which
are seen and temporal, but also at the things which are
not seen and eternal.

PLATO'S BAN UPON POETRY

"AND there shall in no wise enter into it anything that defileth, neither whatsoever worketh abomination or maketh a lie." This sentence of exclusion from the Holy City, New Jerusalem, though expressed with Hebrew intensity rather than with Hellenic restraint, is based upon the same grounds on which Plato, in the *Republic*, banishes "the honey'd muse" of poetry from his ideal city, namely, that it exercises a corrupting influence, and does not give us truth.

Plato's chief contribution, and perhaps his only permanent contribution, to the discussion of aesthetics and literary criticism is his teaching that imagination is linked with emotion; that poetry and art do not appeal to the reasoning or logical faculties but to the feelings and emotions. Thereby, as Bosanquet says, he "laid the foundation of all aesthetic theory."

To Plato's way of thinking, this at once and inevitably put poetry and art on a lower level than science and philosophy. For his psychology did not merely note the difference between reason and the emotions; it included also a scale of values. Of all human powers, Plato ranks reason as highest and supreme, meaning by reason the faculty which, by logical processes, establishes or discovers truth. At its lower stages this faculty regulates conduct by consistent principles (for Plato adhered to the belief of Socrates that con-

duct, to be perfectly virtuous, must be based on consistent principles consciously held, and not on instincts or loyalties or good sense or good taste; that,
to be morally good, one must be able to give a clear
and reasoned account of his principles of conduct).
And at its highest stage, when it has come to its own,
reason gives us a clear and comprehensive grasp of
the universe seen as an ordered whole, a perfect
science and metaphysics in one.   It follows that, as
this is the highest activity of man's supremest faculty,
it must be here that man comes nearest to the divine
activity.   The man after God's own heart is the consummate scientist or philosopher (Plato makes no
such distinction here as we do; the ultimate truth is
one).   The human soul has no window through
which simple-minded and unlettered folk may discover God.   No divine truth is revealed to babes
and sucklings—nor to poets and artists either, since it
is not by logical processes that they produce their
results.

We should note that this conception of scientific
and philosophic insight into truth by the establishment of universal principles was a recent acquisition
of the human mind; in fact, one of the greatest of the
achievements of that amazing fifth century B.C.   To
the development and establishment of this new activity
of the mind Plato himself had contributed enormously,
and in founding his Academy he was the first to conceive of an institution for organized scientific research.
It is no wonder that he jealously defended science and
philosophy from all disparaging attacks, and it is not

unnatural that he should over-estimate the importance of this new approach to truth.

He also at the same time exaggerated the defects of the emotional element and of the arts that make their appeal to the feelings and the imagination. He not merely put them on a lower level than the processes of the logical faculty, and deemed them of less value; they are, he held, dangerous in themselves and apt to be positively harmful. In his view, Reason and Emotion are opposed to each other as if set in the opposite scales of a balance. We cannot serve Reason and Feeling, any more than we can serve God and Mammon.

His argument for this uncompromising hostility is put with less than his usually sound logic, and may, not unfairly, be summarized thus: Science is diametrically opposed to poetry (the quarrel between them is of long standing); but science is also opposed to error and falsity and illusion, which it is the work of science to correct and destroy. Therefore, he argues, since science is opposed to these and also opposed to poetry, poetry must be essentially linked with error and falsity and illusion. Plato virtually assumes as axiomatic that things opposed to the same thing are identical with each other.* And so he emphasizes the contrast between reason and unreason; between truth and error; between clear insight into reality and confusion of mind; between the

* It is as though one were to argue: Faith is opposed to Knowledge; and Faith is also opposed to Doubt and Scepticism. Therefore Knowledge and Scepticism are one and identical.

vision of truth and the State of illusion; as though this contrast corresponded precisely to that between the point of view of the philosopher or scientist and the attitude of the poet. Wordsworth also, like Plato, held that the opposite of poetry is not prose but science, and, in his verses on the grave of Burns, the scientist (under his old name of physician, a Student of nature) is warned not to profane with his approach the poet's grave:

> Physician art thou? one all eyes,
> Philosopher! a fingering slave;
> One that would peep and botanize
> Upon his mother's grave?

Plato would have assented to this view of their incompatibility; but he would have reversed the situation, and would have warned the poet that he was unworthy to draw near the scientist.

Plato saw quite clearly and quite correctly that it is not the office of the emotions to reveal or discover scientific truth; but he assumed too hastily that they could not discover or reveal any truth at all. To him there is but one Truth, and Philosophy is its prophet. More than once he points out that the poet works, not by scientific formulas and logical processes, but by a divine gift and inspiration; and he assumes that, as he does not work by rational principles which he consciously follows and can expound to others, he must be temporarily out of his mind and literally in an *ecstasy*; like an inspired prophet who, under the divine afflatus, utters what is given him to say, without having thought it out by any process of reasoning of

G

his own. We may compare Conrad's reference to "the artist's appeal to that within us which is not a part of wisdom—that which is a gift and not an acquisition." Plato goes much farther, and constantly assumes that as poetry is not, in the strictest sense, rational, it must be irrational; that what, in Conrad's phrase, is not a part of wisdom must belong to the category of the erroneous, the deceitful, the fallacious.

In addition to this first objection, based on his psychology, Plato further justifies his disparagement of poetry and art by an argument connected with his Ideal Theory. To Plato, as to all idealists, the things that are seen are temporal; the eternal can never be seen by the eye of sense. The objects which make up this world of time and space are to him but imperfect copies of eternal realities, which no eye of the flesh can see, but which the mind may be trained to discern. The realm of sense is transitory, full of defects and inconsistencies; the realm of thought is more real and eternal because more permanent and consistent. We constantly oppose the *real* to the *ideal*. To Plato, these are identical; and to them he opposes the *actual*, all that comes and goes in this mortal life of ours, the fleeting shows of time and sense. A recent article in an English review contrasts two conceptions of art. The true business of art, the writer says, is to reveal the eternal through things of time; and over against this he puts what he prefers to call a craft, which, instead of enabling us to discern the real and the eternal, merely portrays actual things. Singularly enough, the writer goes on to speak of the former as the "Platonic" view; whereas Plato makes no such distinction, but unmistakably holds that all art is of precisely the latter kind, the portrayal of the actual, and maintains that it is science and philosophy alone that can reveal the eternal realities that lie behind the things of time.

Plato knows nothing of our distinction between creative (imaginative or idealistic) art and realistic (or photographic) art, and the term he uses, *mimesis*, is wide enough to include both. This word, usually translated by *imitation*, is applied to the artist's or poet's function by Greeks of all periods, including Plato's critic, Aristotle. It has often been said that it was an "unfortunate" word to use, and responsible for much of Plato's wrong-headed attitude. What is really unfortunate is the inadequacy of the English rendering. As a rule, *representation* would be a far better translation, or sometimes *expression*. As applied to a battle, for instance, the word "imitation" suggests only a sham fight; whereas the Greek word would quite naturally and properly be used to express the representation of a battle by a painter (of whatever school) or a musician or a poet (say, *The Charge of the Light Brigade*, or *Scots Wha Hae*). Certainly none of these by his art produces an actual battle; therefore the Greeks assigned what he did produce to *mimesis*. Some of Plato's illustrations, to be sure, are cases of ordinary imitation, but the imitation, as with all art, is in another medium, and is never mere counterfeiting, like "imitation pearls." No, the real source of his error is not the "unfortunate" word *mimesis*, but rather the implications of his Ideal Theory. The conviction that the actual world is an imperfect and impermanent counterpart of the world of eternal realities suggests to him that similarly all art and all poetry, even that which we call creative and idealistic, are in their turn but semblances of the actual, and thus one stage further removed from reality.

It all comes back, ultimately, to Plato's narrowing of the conception of truth and knowledge to the rational processes of the scientist or philosopher. In that sense the artist and the poet never see, and therefore cannot reveal, the eternal through things of time. Plato does not conceive the possibility of any of them having a different kind of vision of some ideal beauty or truth or goodness that lies close to the heart of the Eternal. They see, at best, Shelley's dome of many-coloured glass that stains the white radiance of eternity. Theirs is not the light that never was on sea or land. They merely see that which is open to all eyes to behold, and they have a special gift or skill in giving us a copy of that which is itself but a copy of the eternal and ideal reality, of which only the reason at its highest may hope to catch the vision. That this is not the only conclusion that may be drawn from the theory of eternal Ideas may readily be granted, as the Neo-Platonist Plotinus saw, and Adam is justified in saying that the famous lines of Wordsworth on King's College Chapel, "They dreamt not of a perishable home Who thus could build," are more truly and characteristically Platonic than Plato's attack upon poetry and painting.

Up to a certain point one can agree and sympathize with Plato's insistence that we should "do noble deeds, not dream them." Those are fine words, among the very last he ever wrote: "Sirs, we are ourselves composers of a tragedy, as far as in us lies the noblest and the best. Our State is framed to be a reproduction of the noblest and best life; and that is indeed, as we hold, the noblest tragedy." In plainer prose, in the lives we live and the society we help to build up we are writing the noblest kind of poem. But Plato is carried away by the ardour of his attack too far in the opposite direction, and in the artistic representations of actions and objects he can find nothing at all comparable to the actions and objects themselves. In this he is unlike Tennyson, who wrote, "The song that nerves a nation's heart is in itself a deed," and unlike Schiller, who held that we are not really civilized till we prefer the semblance to the actual. I have long treasured a clipping from an English paper which contains the *reductio ad absurdum* of Plato's contention that Art gives us but an inferior and partial copy of the actual. At a Tailors and Cutters Congress held in London, the president, in his annual address, asked the members: "Why should we be ranked as second to painters and sculptors? Do we not supply the originals for these artists to copy? All they need to do is to reproduce accurately what we have done and their fame is assured." That is precisely the point of view of the tenth book of the *Republic*.

Plato's objection to poetry was powerfully reinforced by still another consideration. He profoundly distrusted the emotions, and condemned whatever roused or nourished them, not merely for theoretical reasons, but from practical experience. The Greek, and particularly the Athenian Greek, was excitable by nature, like most southern European peoples. Plato repreatedly remarks on the lack of moral steadiness and balance which he observed in the Athenian citizen as contrasted with the Spartan, who in some respects resembled the typical John Bull as contrasted with the "flighty French." He deplores the lack of restraint, the volatility, the quick response to anything sensational and novel that he found in his countrymen; and, therefore, to such a people he preaches repression of feeling and emotion—a doctrine which, to our more undemonstrative northern temperament, seems to savour of ultra - Puritanic asceticism. He was not, however, urging the Englishman to be more like an iceberg; he was merely trying to make the Athenian less inflammable.

Interested supremely as he was in the upbuilding of the noblest life among his countrymen, in their moral, as well as in their intellectual, growth, he distrusted the poetry, and especially the drama, which makes so strong an appeal to emotion; what his people needed was rather to learn to curb their tendency to go to extremes in the expression of intense feeling. For he saw quite as clearly as Aristotle that the sphere of the dramatic art is where action is accompanied by emotion; and not emotion under firm control, but emotion finding full expression. He notes how hard it is to make a convincing and attractive picture in poetry of a thoroughly good character or of a life lived under quite normal, and therefore (theoretically) desirable conditions. "A good woman," said a great modern actress, "is a dramatic impossibility." Thackeray meant Amelia Sedley to be the beau-ideal of womanhood, but it is Becky Sharp, not Amelia Sedley, who lingers in our memory. And neither Virgil's Aeneas nor Tennyson's King Arthur succeeds in winning our whole-hearted admiration for his goodness. It is difficult, argues Plato (and experience confirms it), for a dramatist to make good people interesting; it is much easier to make bad people interesting. But to portray wholly undesirable people and experiences so interestingly and so insidiously Plato held to be fraught with danger. Under the poet's spell we enter into the very minds and feelings of people whom we should not care to resemble, and by imaginative sympathy we make them our own; and, because it is all imaginary and make-believe, our suspicions are lulled. We are caught off our guard, and, without being aware of it, we tend to become assimilated to the characters that for the time being have absorbed us. Thus we are taken out of ourselves, and are, therefore, less able to develop our own true selves and play our own proper part in life. These characters of the poet are not necessarily all vicious characters; they may be quite good people, but in their less admirable moments when they fall distinctly below their own best standard. But, good or bad, they are always people who, at the time, are excited, passionate, sorrowing, exulting, with much less restraint than we should care to show ourselves.

Such was Plato's argument. Can we say that he was wholly wrong in thinking that for his mercurial countrymen, eager for sensation and prone to excessive emotionalism, what was most needed was not the drama they so loved, but something that would steady them and calm their lively, excitable temperaments?

This also is to be remembered in trying to understand why Plato excluded the poets from his ideal city. He had to defend science and philosophy against those who attacked all this "new learning" and decried his attempt to attain sure and complete knowledge by these new methods. Science and philosophy, it was charged, are useless and visionary; poetry, especially the great national epics of Homer, will furnish all the guidance and enlightenment that people need. Shelley called poets the unacknowledged legislators of the world. But it was not so in Greece; there they were the recognized authority on life and its problems. Homer has often been called the "Bible of the Greeks." Greek youths were brought up on Homer as, a few decades ago, a Scottish boy was brought up on the Bible and the Shorter Catechism. They learned large portions of Homer by heart, and they were taught to find in his characters their ideals of manliness and all desirable qualities. It was Homer, with one or two lesser poets, that above all other influences moulded the character of the Greeks and shaped their conceptions of "life and the things beyond life." So

great a poet as Homer, writing on so grand a scale,
seemed also to his admirers to possess all knowledge.
Similarly, every little while, someone comes forward
to claim for Shakespeare personal and complete
familiarity with this or that craft or calling. "He
must have known all about it, to describe it so well,"
it is felt.   So the Greeks discovered in Homer all the
arts and sciences man could need, and the new search
for knowledge in Plato's Academy was regarded by
many as superfluous if not impertinent.

The proper course, we should be inclined to say,
would be to find room for both, to welcome equally
the inspiration and enjoyment to be derived from
poetry and the enlightenment that comes from science
and philosophy.   But neither Plato nor Plato's critics
would have it so.   Each side claimed all merit for its
own preference and saw no value in any other.   Each
side, the advocates of poetry and the advocates of
philosophy alike, believed, as it were, that it possessed
a complete food which omitted none of the elements
desirable for perfect health, and would admit no
nutritive value in its rival.   Bosanquet ingeniously
compares the rival theories that exist to-day about
the Bible.   Some hold that it speaks with authority
upon every department of life, so that we can find in
it the final word on every topic.   Others charge
that it is not in agreement with the ascertained truths
of science, and is therefore valueless.   The third, and
most sensible, view is that it is not a scientific treatise,
but has a special sphere of its own, and in its proper
sphere has inestimable value.

Plato's quarrel with poetry, and especially with dramatic poetry, is largely due, as we have seen, to his conceiving it as an imaginative and sympathetic portrayal of moods and feelings that in one's own experience would not be thought desirable. It is probable that in his day the drama might fairly be called degenerate, or at least degenerating. He quite evidently did not care for Euripides, the sentimentalist, and it is to Euripides that his strictures usually apply, and not to the two other great dramatists of the previous century. Euripides is a master of emotional effects; he can harrow our feelings and pluck at our very heart's strings in isolated scenes as no other ancient writer can—often at the expense of the unity and perfection of the play as a whole. But the mere stirring of emotion for the sake of emotion is the last thing Plato was likely to approve in that day and among that people; and therefore he excludes all such poetry from the New Jerusalem he so zealously, all his life long, was trying to build among men.

Plato, however, did not propose to abolish absolutely all poetry or banish all poets. In fact, his condemnation of such poetry as he would exclude is but the reverse side of a very lofty conception of the place poetry might, and should, occupy in the life of man. The poet is to be no longer "the idle singer of an empty day," and still less the corrupter and seducer of the souls of men. He is to compose for the State its hymns to the gods and the *encomia* of its heroes. And under the ever-watchful supervision of the philosopher kings of Plato's ideal commonwealth, poetry

and imaginative fiction will present to the plastic minds
of youth noble examples for it to emulate (for assimilation through the imagination to what is upright and
heroic is wholly commendable), and will, moreover,
for the mass of citizens clothe in forms suited to their
grasp the high truths they are not philosophic enough
to apprehend. And thus the citizens will be sur-
rounded always by salutary influences, "like breezes
bringing health from a wholesome environment."

To Plato's high conception of the office of the true
poet Nettleship well compares that set forth in Milton's lofty and sonorous prose (though Milton would
have repudiated Plato's idea of a rigid censorship of
literature by the philosophic guardians of his State):
"to inbreed and cherish in a great people the seeds of
virtue and public civility; to allay the perturbations of
the mind and set the affections in right tune; to celebrate in glorious and lofty hymns the throne and
equipage of God's almightiness; . . . lastly, whatsoever in religion is holy and sublime, in virtue amiable
or grave, whatsoever hath passion or admiration in all
the changes of fortune from without, or the wily sub-
tleties of man's thoughts from within; all these things,
with a solid and treatable smoothness, to point out
and describe."

Thus, if Plato is a severe censor of poetry, it is
because he invites it to occupy so high a place in
human life. He offers it a noble office, and would
not have it descend to any lower level or be content
with ignoble or petty aims. The poetry that is merely
for the enjoyment of the idle moment, the poetry that

reflects the trivial sentiments and the less heroic moods
of the soul—this poetry Plato finds not merely valueless but dangerous to his countrymen. With the mere
littérateur, also, the dilettante, the sentimentalist, the
delicate taster of *belles-lettres*, he would have as little
sympathy as Ruskin, who once complained: "I tell
people their plain duty, and they say what a beautiful
style I have."

Plato, who is perhaps the greatest prose writer
European civilization has ever known, is himself too
consummate a literary artist for us to imagine for a
moment that his hostility is due to any insensibility
to the charm of fine poetry. That charm he feels and
freely acknowledges. But certain principles which
he cannot but regard as fundamental and incontro-
vertible lead logically and necessarily, he believes,
to the condemnation he is reluctantly compelled to
utter. "At any cost we must follow reason where it
leads us." Nevertheless, while he excludes poetry
from his ideal State, and shows the poet the door,
dismissing him with all respect and courtesy, to be
sure, and yet inexorably, almost his last utterance on
the subject in the *Republic* is to agree that poetry may
be readmitted if she can make an adequate defence
and prove her worth. Poetry's own plea would, of
course, be couched in verse; but, he proceeds, "to
those also of her advocates who love poetry and yet
are not themselves poets, permission will be given
to uphold her cause in prose, and show that she not
only gives pleasure but is also helpful to communities
and in the life of man; and we shall listen in a friendly

spirit, for it will be clear gain if it is proved that poetry is helpful as well as delightful." This offer, or challenge, was accepted by Aristotle in the *Poetics*, not literally or explicitly, of course, but virtually so. Plato's disparagement of poetry and art as a mere copy of external and sensible things or actions is corrected by Aristotle's truer conception of the nature of *mimesis* or artistic portrayal, as something into which a universal element may enter; and Plato's fear that poetry corrupts, by undesirably awakening the emotions and feelings and thus strengthening the lower part of man's nature, is answered by Aristotle's doctrine that a true tragedy is a tonic * that restores the soul to health and vigour.

* Perhaps an apology is due for substituting for Aristotle's obsolete and obscure medical metaphor of *katharsis* a more modern one which would seem to convey the same general purport.

PLATO AND JOB

OF the two names, Plato and Job, which form the subject of this paper, it would be hard to say which is the more famous, or which will live longer in human memory.

In the whole range of European civilization, no one stands higher than Plato as a consummate literary artist, a profound thinker, and a perennial fount of inspiration to the Western mind. The range of his interests and of his influence is amazing. Take up any important modern work dealing with the fundamental problems of philosophy or theology or psychology or education, political or ethical science, the theory of art, or the principles of literary criticism, and turn to the index; the chances are that the references to Plato will be found outstanding, and often outnumbering all other names. "Out of Plato," said Emerson, "come all things that are still written and debated among men of thought." Or, as another writer has expressed it: "Plato has taught us what are the great questions to ask." Most of these questions the world of thought is still asking, and there are few of them on which Plato's views and their implications are not still well worth considering.

The *Book of Job*, again, as part of the English Bible, is probably far more widely read than Plato, and has been the subject of quite as many commentators and interpreters. Owing, however, to the faulty translation of the Authorized Version, it has been, and still is, widely misunderstood. No other part of the Bible gains so much from being read in the Revised Version; but great and important difficulties still remain, and on some of the chief points of controversy, agreement may never, perhaps, be reached. While, as compared with Plato, the range of subject-matter in the *Book of Job* is narrow, yet the moving eloquence, the sublimity of vision, and the passionate intensity with which one of the deepest and most persistent problems of universal humanity is set forth, mark it out as one of the few really great books of the world.

In view of the magnitude of the field, it may seem the height of presumption to undertake within the compass of a short paper to deal with two such writers. "Canst thou draw out leviathan with an hook?" is asked of Job, in scorn of his limitations. How much less may I, with my puny hook, expect to cope with two leviathans?

But, in fact, it greatly lessens my task to combine the two as I am doing. For the ground common to them, the space where their widely different orbits intersect and leave a certain segment which belongs to both, is relatively small and manageable. There is but one problem with which they are both concerned; everything else, however important and however interesting in itself, may be disregarded. The one subject which they both discuss consists of the difficulties and questionings that arise from the apparent discrepancy in this life of ours between merit and reward, between the prosperity of the wicked and the suffering that so often falls to the lot of the upright and innocent.

The question of these perplexing providences is central to the *Book of Job*, and, manifold as are the various themes discussed in Plato's greatest work, the *Republic*, it is this problem which gives to it a certain unity. All the other themes there discussed we must ignore, as also we must leave to one side the difficult problems of interpretation with which the *Book of Job* still bristles. All that I hope to do is to call attention as clearly as I can to certain comparisons and contrasts between the two writers in the treatment of their common problem, in the belief that this may prove both interesting and instructive.*

The first point to be noticed is the way in which this problem arose. History seldom really repeats itself, and similar as the problem of Plato's *Republic* and that of the *Book of Job* may appear, they emerged in quite different ways.

For long generations in Israel, Jehovah was preeminently the national God. His covenant was with the nation, not with the individual. The nation as a whole was to be rewarded or punished according to its observance of that covenant; the individual was absorbed and lost in the national destiny. Moreover, the blessings promised and the penalties threatened

---

* All reference to the wider and more fundamental issue of the existence of evil in the world is omitted altogether. It is not a question present to the mind of Job at all; and while Plato has his own views upon the matter as part of his philosophy of the universe, these form no part of his discussion of our particular problem.

were regularly conceived as material and temporal, as
is apparent throughout every portion of the Old
Testament, as, for example, in the long recital in
Deuteronomy xxviii of the blessings and curses pronounced by Moses. By the sixth century, however,
when the national life had been shattered by conquest
and exile, a new conception of the individual's relation to God had arisen. Both Jeremiah and Ezekiel
proclaimed a new message, asserting individual,
instead of national and corporate, responsibility to
God. In this conviction, they tell their people:
"They shall say no more, The fathers have eaten a
sour grape and the children's teeth are set on edge,
but every one shall die for his own iniquity." And
this doctrine, that the righteousness of the righteous
and the wickedness of the wicked shall be upon himself, Ezekiel expands into a whole chapter (xviii). In
one respect, however, there was no change. The
blessings and the punishments that were to result
were still ordinarily conceived in terms of material
prosperity, here and now. The belief in a future life
was not as yet part of the pious Israelite's creed.

But in time doubts began to arise in reflecting
minds. Previously, under the theory of corporate
responsibility, exact correspondence between an individual's acts and his good or evil fortune was not
required or looked for. The punishment brought
about by the disobedience of the nation as a whole, or
of some part of it, might fall upon any of its members,
even in later generations, and not necessarily on the
particular persons guilty of offence. But now that

H

the new doctrine was preached that "the soul that sinneth, it shall die and not another," it could be seen that this theory did not always work; that too often the individual evildoer prospered, and too often the righteous individual failed to obtain the reward promised for his obedience. Here and there in the Psalms, most notably in Psalm lxxiii, one finds the writer disquieted because of the undeserved prosperity of the wicked. In a similar vein, Jeremiah ventures to question the Lord's judgments: "Wherefore doth the way of the wicked prosper? Wherefore are all they happy that deal very treacherously?" But it is only in the *Book of Job* that the voice of the troubled doubter becomes fully articulate. To the orthodox teaching of the Psalmist: "Whatsoever the godly man doeth shall prosper; the ungodly are not so, but are like the chaff which the wind driveth away," Job virtually replies: "That is simply not true; it is not in accordance with the facts of life." Job's friends represent the orthodox belief of the Hebrews at that period, that suffering is punishment for sin; and they therefore argue, quite logically from their premises, that Job's misfortunes must be wholly due to some transgression of God's law. Job himself is conscious that no conduct of his can account for his accumulated misfortunes, and he, therefore, naturally refuses to listen to their exhortations to repent of his presumed sin, and thus again win God's favour. Instead of repenting, he does not hesitate to arraign the injustice of God's dealings with him, and to impeach the moral government of the world. This is done, not out of irreverence, as his shocked friends suppose, but because of his firm resolve to rest satisfied with none but a God of perfect justice and righteousness. His conviction of what God ought to be leads him to repudiate and condemn what God seems to be.

Let us turn now from the Orient to Greece, where the fifth century witnessed an amazing outburst of the human spirit which has nothing in later Western history comparable with it in brilliance and lasting significance, save only the era of the Renaissance and the achievements of the century preceding the Great War. In many matters of permanent human interest that century saw an unprecedented fermentation of ideas and a glorious fruition in such diverse spheres, for example, as medicine, fine art, mathematics, literature, and political theory. Among the new developments which proved of permanent value to mankind was the discussion of the principles governing human society and human conduct, as portrayed for us by the great tragedians and historians of Athens, and more fully in the conversations which Plato (himself a consummate dramatist and prose-poet) attributes to Socrates and his contemporaries.

It would seem that every age is apt to be influenced in the form its thinking takes by some conception of which it has become acutely conscious, and which impresses it as a useful key to unlock the doors of knowledge. Since Darwin's day, men have been alert to trace the evolution of all kinds of institutions and beliefs; the distinction between objective and subjective for a time pervaded all reflective writing; and of late years we have had a surfeit of explanations of human conduct in terms of Freudian complexes and inhibitions, of extroverts and introverts, and all the rest of the jargon of the fashionable psychology of the moment.

So, in fifth-century Athens, the opposition between nature and convention cropped up everywhere in discussions about morality and the basis of the distinction between right and wrong. For one thing, as the Greek became better acquainted with distant lands and foreign peoples, he found great variety in customs and standards, what one nation approved being often reprobated by another. And so the question began to be raised and debated, not by philosophers only, but by the ordinary citizen: Are right and wrong something fixed by nature and unchangeable by human will, or is morality merely a convention, an accepted custom, a more or less unstable fashion? And what of the State also, whose usage and authority determined for the Greek what was held to be right or wrong? Whence comes the State's authority, and what validity do its sanctions possess? Thus essentially, in spite of certain variations, Rousseau and Hobbes and Nietzsche have but repeated in modern times theories that were mooted in Athens more than two thousand years before.

In Plato's *Republic*, in the first of its ten books, it is boldly contended by Thrasymachus that right and wrong are merely what the strongest man or the strongest party in a community ordain, and that, too, purely out of self-interest; everywhere Might is Right,

and law and order have no other basis than "the good
old rule, the simple plan, that they should take who
have the power, and they should keep who can."
Thrasymachus, while a blustering talker, is but a
shallow thinker, and Socrates has no great difficulty
in exposing the contradictions in his arguments.
The thesis, of course, is not itself disproved by the
inadequacies of a weak advocate, and, in the second
book, two young men who were present, brothers of
Plato, tell Socrates that, while they do not themselves
accept these upsetting new doctrines, they think
Thrasymachus's case might have been better argued.
They propose to restate it, in the hope that Socrates
may be able so to refute it as to dispel all possible
doubt.

It might be argued, they say, that in the state of
nature there is everywhere a struggle for survival and
supremacy, the stronger reaping the fruits of victory,
the weaker going to the wall.   But experience showed
that in such a conflict, where every man's hand is
against every other man, each combatant is in a hope-
less minority, and is much more likely to be a victim
than a successful survivor. So, they suggest, an
agreement was somehow arrived at that all should
abstain from ruthless aggression and should respect
one another's claims.   Here, then, lies the origin of
law and ordered society, of justice and morality; not
in the dictates of nature, but in this compact and com-
promise.   It results, therefore, that the law-abiding life
is but a second best.   It is much better, of course, than
being the helpless sufferer from another's aggression,

but also it is much less desirable than being one-
self the successful aggressor, hampered by no scruples
and withheld by no obstacles from pursuing solely his
own interest. Any one, therefore, with the strength
and the opportunity to override or evade the restrictions of law and morality would be a fool if he failed
to do so and was content to abide by the conventional
code. It may be true that usually, and for most men,
"honesty is the best policy," but if at any time one
can see his way to get better results by dishonesty,
why should he remain honest? To be unscrupulous,
selfish, and dishonest is but obeying nature, if only
one can "get away with it"; to adhere to conventional morality and be scrupulously honest argues one
a fool or a weakling. The great thing is to obtain
wealth and power and fame; both honesty and dishonesty are no more than possible means to the
desired end, and which of them will, in any given
case, bring one nearer success depends wholly on
circumstances.

In support of this view, they point out how much
of the orthodox recommendation of virtue and
honesty by both parents and professional moralists
is, after all, based on purely prudential grounds;
virtue is praised because of its rewards. It is a fair
inference that even its advocates do not think morality
desirable for its own sake, but merely the best way, on
the whole, of getting the worldly success and repute
which are the real objects of desire. One thinks of
the prudential counsels to godliness which abound in
the Old Testament, such as, "Honour thy father and

thy mother that thy days may be long," or "Length of days is in her right hand, and in her left hand riches and honour."   Such, too, is the naïve vow of Jacob at Bethel: "If God will be with me . . . and will give me bread to eat and raiment to put on, so that I come again to my father's house in peace, then shall the Lord be my God."   Jacob might well regard this as a good bargain to make.

To return to Plato, the upshot is that Socrates is challenged by the two brothers to prove that uprightness is to be chosen for its own sake, and wholly apart from any reward or reputation that may attach to it.   Two pictures are drawn: one of a wicked man prospering all his days in his wickedness, absolutely efficient and no "bungler" in his unscrupulousness, so that by craft or power he is able to gain complete impunity and is honoured and envied by all about him.   Then over against him they depict a wholly just and upright man, misunderstood by his fellows so as to suffer always the penalties of an undeserved evil reputation; the best of men in reality, but looked on as a vile knave; and so continuing till his death, it may be an undeserved and cruel death by scourging, the rack, or crucifixion (literally, impaling).   "If this passage were found in the Old Testament, it would have been considered a Messianic prophecy," says Constantin Ritter, and a reference Bible would perhaps compare Isaiah's chapter (liii) on the Suffering Servant.

Prove to us, the brothers then demand of Socrates, that if we are wise we shall choose to be the latter of these two men rather than the former.   In other words, show us that Job, at the height of his misfortunes, was infinitely better off, just because of his integrity and uprightness, than the rich but wicked men of whose prosperity he complains. If Socrates cannot prove that, they hold that they would be justified in assuming that virtue has no intrinsic worth, but is at best a means (and not necessarily always the best means) of obtaining worldly success. As, in a modern scientific experiment, care is taken to eliminate every factor that might vitiate the result, so Socrates is required to leave out of consideration material prosperity and adversity, reputation, physical suffering—everything but goodness and wickedness of soul, in order that the intrinsic value of these may be determined. And manifestly the way to ensure an incontestable verdict is to give the wicked man every material and temporal advantage, and to load the upright man with adversity, ill repute, and suffering.

Thus, by quite different paths, the Hebrew and the Greek writer have both come to face the problem presented by the unmerited prosperity of the wicked and the undeserved misfortunes of the innocent. And yet, if we look closely, we shall find that the problem raised is not really identical for the two thinkers. What really engages their interest is quite different. In Hebrew thought, morality was closely connected with religion and signified obedience to the expressed commands of Jehovah. In Greece, morality had little to do with religion; it was more a matter of good citizenship and of one's duties to his fellow-citizens, and in each community it was based upon observance of the community's traditional usages. For the Israelite, the fountain-head of morality was the God of his fathers; for the Greek, the ways of his fathers. Correspondingly, as we shall see, Job's problem was a religious problem, Plato's a social and political problem.

In this inquiry Plato is chiefly concerned with the question how life in the community would be affected by the new theory that was abroad, the theory that the rules of moral conduct have no natural validity but are matters of convenience and accommodation. The issue raised was a vitally practical one and no mere academic theme. That age was like our own in witnessing a marked decline of the time-honoured morality and a serious loosening of the hold upon society of the accepted standards of right and wrong. One of the brothers pictures the young men of Athens, especially those whose abilities and resources marked them out for eminence and leadership, debating within themselves, as they faced their future career, which rule of life to adopt; whether it would pay them best to follow the safe but unalluring road of humdrum acquiescence in conventional morality, or to give reins to their ambition and seek the career to which nature herself seems to call those who are strong and capable. If the only question for the potential Alcibiades or Critias is: Which course will it be more profitable to follow? there is grave danger that he will make a choice dangerous alike to the community and to himself. The situation demanded a surer knowledge and a clearer insight than the ordinary guides and guardians of youth possessed, and Plato, in this, the greatest of his dialogues, devotes his best energies to putting into the mouth of Socrates a convincing vindication of justice and uprightness as against unscrupulous self-seeking.

Something like this may seem to breathe in the words of Job (xxi) when he is speaking of the wicked who live, become old, yea, wax mighty in power; whose houses are safe from fear, who spend their days in prosperity and go down to the grave in peace; and then represents such people as asking: "What is the Almighty that we should serve Him? and what profit should we have if we pray to Him?" But what really disturbs Job is not what God's silence may suggest to the evil-doer, and the consequent danger to society, but what His silence implies to the afflicted righteous man, whom God seems to have forgotten, who dies in bitterness of soul, and never tastes of the good which God, if He were really a God of justice, would have bestowed upon him. Job is in despair because God now hides Himself from him and vouchsafes no answer to his appeals and remonstrances; and, in his despair at the loss of the former Divine favour and fellowship, he begins to doubt God's justice. In brief, Job is concerned above all with man's relations with God, while Plato's concern is with man's relations with his fellow-men.

This is in complete harmony with a difference between the Greek and the Hebrew attitude to life that has often been remarked, as in the following apposite passage: "In their approach to the problem

of life, the two civilizations start at opposite ends.
Greece starts at the human end [and works] from the
seen to the unseen. Palestine begins at the opposite
end and works from God down to man. Super-
ficially the results appear the same. Though [Plato]
starts with man, he reaches God. His ethics begin
with psychology, but end in religion. But for Plato,
theism is a deduction from his view of the world, not
the prime reality with which he begins. The Bible
has a different attitude. Whereas God is a conclusion to the Greek, to the Hebrew he is the main
premise. Hence a difference of emphasis. The real
subject of Greek literature is man. . . . The subject
of the Bible, on the other hand, is not man, but God,
and every page bears witness to what is uppermost in
the writers' minds."

So much, then, for the problem itself. But before
turning to its solution, let us first refer to a relevant
and long-debated point in the interpretation of the
Book of Job. To what extent does Job believe in a
life beyond the grave, where, if not here, he may
receive justice and final vindication? The evidence,
especially in the Authorized Version, seems to point
two ways. One famous passage gave Handel the
words of the triumphant aria so familiar to us at
Easter-tide, "I know that my Redeemer liveth."
(But of this passage practically all scholars to-day give
a quite different interpretation from the time-honoured
one.) On the other hand, there are many passages

in the book in which Job seems to share the belief
current in Israel until a much later period, that the soul,
a dim, shadowy, quasi-material thing, goes at death
to Sheol, the grave or pit, where all the dead alike are
gathered without distinction of rank or character, and
where there is no manifestation of life or thought or
feeling; very like the unsubstantial underworld of the
Homeric Hades. Happily, we do not need to go into
the question at any length. For our present purpose
it is sufficient to say that the utmost any one is dis-
posed to contend for is that the sudden thought of a
conceivable vindication in the future flashes before
the mind of Job and, for a moment, lightens his
gloom. But any such fitful gleams of hope are
swiftly followed by blank despair and hopelessness.
He is not sustained by any firm belief or steadfast hope
that in a future life the inequalities of this mortal
existence are made good. It is here, in this present
life, that righteousness should triumph and be rewarded, if Job is to be convinced of God's justice.

Plato, on the other hand, had a firm and definite
faith in the immortality of the soul, much nearer our
understanding of that phrase than anything discoverable in the Old Testament, and his conception
of it includes a righteous judgment of the souls of
men after death, and an assurance for the good of a
life beyond the grave far more satisfying than this
transitory mortal existence can ever be. And yet
in this inquiry to which Socrates is challenged any
such consideration is rigorously excluded. The problem of the respective value of a just and of an unjust

life must not be complicated by any possibility of
rewards and punishments in a future life, any more
than by rewards and punishments in this present life.
For what Plato is going to try to establish is that, even
with all the inequalities here and now that can be conceived of, and even if death ends all, yet even so, if
our eyes were opened to see the truth, we should
unhesitatingly pronounce the most afflicted just man
to be infinitely better off, here and now, than the most
prosperous and triumphant unjust man.   Plato, that
is, is ready to concede this topsy-turvy world that
so distresses Job, and also to disregard all possibility
of that future life which would have consoled Job,
and yet undertakes to establish the superior felicity
of the righteous man, solely because of his righteousness.

How, then, does Plato propose to maintain this
remarkable thesis?   As the best life for any creature
must be in harmony with its own particular nature, it
follows that we must know what sort of being man
really is, in order to determine under what conditions
he will attain to complete satisfaction and felicity.
Plato, therefore, begins with an investigation into the
nature of man by analysing the various potentialities
and aspirations in man that seek realization and satisfaction.   This analysis of human nature leads Plato
far afield; for, whatever else be true of man, it is
manifest that he is made for association with his fellow-
men in some sort of common life with others; and,
accordingly, a large part of the *Republic* is devoted to
a discussion of the sort of community in which the

individual can best find the life he was meant to live.*
Those in our day who are demanding a new social
order, as a condition precedent, are (to that extent, at
least) good Platonists. This description by Plato of
what he believed to be the best form of community
life is the first of Utopias, as it is also the most eloquent
and the most profound. In this way Plato's inquiry
becomes as much political as ethical, a distinction that
would mean little or nothing to him; and we may also
call it psychological, inasmuch as it involves an analysis
of man's infinitely complex nature.

What, then, does this analysis disclose? The most
obvious component is the desire for food and shelter
and other satisfactions desirable simply because we
have a body. But Plato would assent to Burke's contention that our life is "not a partnership in things
subservient only to the gross animal existence of a
temporary and perishable nature," but is "a partnership in all science, a partnership in all art, a partnership in every virtue and in all perfection." And so
he proceeds to marshal in due order other aspects of
human nature which call for satisfactions other than
mere creature comforts. First are those which reveal
themselves in our conduct and character, in our relations with our fellows. Afterwards follow our desire
for knowledge and our capacity for speculation and research, in a word, our intellectual and spiritual aspira-

* It is this feature that has given rise to the name *Republic* for this
dialogue. The Greek word it translates, like the Latin word *respublica*,
has nothing to do with what we call a republican form of government,
but is applicable to any organized community; and both the principles
of government in any community and its social order are alike covered
by the word so translated.

tions for the good, the true, and the beautiful. Thus
his survey covers the whole gamut from the infant's
instinctive reactions up to the seer's Vision of God,
from our perception of the things that are seen and
temporal to our reaching out after the things that are
unseen and eternal.

This survey, which is long and intricate, extending
over several books, does not stop with merely cata-
loguing the various constituents of human nature.
Plato also seeks to establish a standard and scale of
values, whether it be in the inner aspects of the soul or
in the objects to which they are directed. Here we need
notice only his results, and not his arguments. Lowest
of all he puts the "appetitive" part directed to the
acquisition of food and material goods and to the
satisfaction of desires which we share with the animal
creation. Above these are all the qualities which
raise man above the brute, highest of all being the
power which may be developed in man of apprehend-
ing eternal verities, and entering into communion with
the divine in the universe, by virtue of man's having
in himself something of divine nature and origin.
What we call the moral life of man consists largely
in the regulation of the lower animal-like appetites
by the higher and diviner powers, and is not ranked
as high by Plato as the pure exercise of these diviner
powers in "thinking God's thoughts after him."

This analysis is the earliest attempt at a systematic
psychology that has come down to us, and, like all
first beginnings, is necessarily tentative and incom-
plete, though a surprisingly large part of it has stood

the test of time. Plato's scale of values, as distinct
from the analysis proper, would, of course, not be
accepted by those to-day who not merely recognize
the part played by the subconscious and the unconscious, the impulsive and instinctive, but greatly over-
emphasize it, and who sometimes seem to be out-
doing the French revolutionists, who set up the Goddess of Reason, by enthroning for our homage the
Goddess of Unreason. Nor, again, would all Plato's
persuasive magic carry weight with those of our
youthful intelligentsia who have taken D. H. Law-
rence to their hearts and applaud his exaltation of the
"guts and genitals" as the prime source of all that is
most precious in life and literature.

But, if the supremacy of mind and reason over the
emotions and the appetites is admitted, Plato is now
ready for the final step in his long argument. If man,
he points out, is to be really man, enjoying true well-
being in accordance with his natural constitution, all
parts of his being must function fully and harmoniously.
For Plato is too genuine a Greek to be an ascetic, and
he believes that nothing that nature intended for use
should be mortified or atrophied, as if it were something common and unclean. But, at the same time
also, every activity, every spring of action must be
under the direction and control of that diviner element, the reason, which alone can understand nature's
intentions for man and plan for their fulfilment.
Only thus can there be true and permanent satisfaction
for the whole man and for each part of him. Plato's
thought is comparable with the great saying of St

Augustine: "Thou hast made us for Thyself, and our hearts are restless until they find rest in Thee." Each of them believes that to miss the life we were constituted for spells misery and disaster, and each believes that human nature, in the sense of man as he was meant to be, partakes in the endowments of the divine nature.

This harmony of the inner life, of which uprightness and justice are one important phase, is then shown to be akin to health in the body as being its true, natural, and only tolerable condition, while disharmony or disorganization is like disease; and in the wicked there *is* disorganization of soul proportionate to their wickedness, for there the noblest and divinest elements that were meant to rule are more and more enslaved to appetites and passions which it is in our true interest to keep in subjection. Then, in one of Plato's most notable similes, man, with all his varied powers and springs of action, is compared to an imagined composite creature, which has the outward semblance of a man, but within includes, along with a human being, many animals, wild and tame, noble and ignoble.

With this comparison in our minds, we are finally asked: What can it profit a man to gain unjustly all the gold in the world, if thereby he is selling his divinest part, which is his true self, into slavery and subjection to the very grossest and most bestial part? a question which cannot but suggest a similar inquiry in the New Testament. Hugh Price Hughes once wrote in his *Social Christianity*: "Christ declares that all the prizes of this world are mere refuse in comparison

I

with the life of the soul.   Now all this was new.
. . . It had never been uttered before Christ came.
He was the first public teacher in this world who said
that man's true worth was to be determined, not by
his property, not by his social position, but solely and
entirely by what he was in himself, by his mind and by
his heart."   Mr Hughes was wrong, whether through
ignorance or excess of zeal, does not appear.   That
was precisely the teaching which Plato often attributes
to Socrates, and to establish this thesis was one of the
main objects in writing the *Republic*.

Plato's answer, then, to the problem which the two
brothers asked Socrates to solve, may be put thus:
The true punishment of wickedness is not loss of
wealth or of reputation or of life itself, nor endless
pain hereafter, nor even the stings and reproach of
conscience,* but it is the disease and deterioration of

* The reason for including in this statement the reference to the
reproach or approval of conscience (which are not specifically mentioned by Plato) is this.   Many years ago a striking magazine article
appeared from the pen of an eminent Old Country writer, in which
Job's problem was set forth in terms of modern life.   Several solu-
tions were suggested only to be set aside as not wholly satisfactory.
(All of these, it should be said, had been already dismissed by Plato
also.)   The writer's final suggestion was that, even without waiting
for a future life to adjust the balance between Dives and Lazarus (who
in this article represent Plato's two contrasted characters), the accounts
are in reality being squared here and now.   "Is it absolutely certain,"
he asks, "that Dives rejoices?   What of the gnawing misery of self-
contempt, of the conscious impoverishment of the soul?"   It is, of
course, undeniable that where these are present, the prosperity of the
wicked has turned to Dead Sea apples; but are they always and
inevitably present?   May not a wicked man quite conceivably go
through life to the day of his death complacent and exulting, and not
at all conscious of any impoverishment of his soul?   Strike out the
word "conscious," and we get precisely Plato's view, that the real
and inescapable punishment (*whether perceived or not*) is the impoverishment of the soul, the disastrous and awful failure to realize man's high
possibilities.

the soul, whereby man has missed becoming what he might have been; and, on the other hand, the true reward of righteousness is not houses or lands or good repute or a good conscience or eternal joy; whether these be present or not, there is abundant reward in being righteous, for then only is one the man he was meant to be, then only is his truest self in good health and satisfied with fullness of life.

What now have we in the *Book of Job* to set over against this careful and prolonged examination by Plato of the problem they both face, and over against the solution which he proposes? At the first blush the answer would seem to be: Nothing, absolutely nothing. On closer examination, we may find that that answer should be modified.

In any event, there is nothing in the nature of a detailed logical discussion of the problem which has been so vividly presented. That would be wholly alien to the Semitic mind. Livingstone's words have already been quoted, that the Hebrew mind works from God to man. We may go farther than that. There are no intermediate steps or stages conceived between God and man, as there are none between God and external nature. The Semitic mind is quite incurious about the processes by which natural phenomena are brought about; it looks through and past all intermediate stages directly to the great first cause. God commanded, and there was light. For the earthquake and the volcano it is a sufficient explanation that: "He looketh on the earth and it trembleth, he toucheth the hills and they smoke."

An amusing and enlightening illustration of this Semitic attitude is given by Layard, the excavator of Nineveh and Babylon.   He quotes a letter written by a Moslem *cadi*, or judge, resident in a certain Eastern city, about whose population, commerce, and antiquities a Western friend of his had sought information. This is part of the answer:

"MY ILLUSTRIOUS FRIEND AND JOY OF MY LIVER!

"The thing you ask of me is both difficult and useless. Although I have passed all my years in this place, I have neither counted the houses nor have I inquired into the number of the inhabitants; and as to what one person loads on his mules and the other stows away in the bottom of his ship, that is no business of mine.   But, above all, as to the previous history of this city, God only knows the amount of dirt and confusion that the infidels may have eaten before the coming of the sword of Islam. It were unprofitable for us to inquire into it.

"Oh, my soul, oh, my lamb!   Seek not after the things which concern thee not.

"Listen, oh, my son!   There is no wisdom equal unto the belief in God.   He created the world, and shall we liken ourselves unto Him in seeking to penetrate into the mysteries of His creation?   Shall we say, behold this star spinneth round that star, and this other star with a tail goeth and cometh in so many years?   Let it go!   He from whose hand it came will guide and direct it."

No, we need not look in Hebrew literature for scientific investigation or for philosophical discussion. Where the Greek (and, thanks to Greek influence, the western world) seeks to know, to analyse, to discuss, and to define, the Hebrew bows in reverent awe before an unsearchable mystery.   All the speakers in the *Book of Job*, however they may differ in other matters, agree in this attitude.   "Canst thou by searching find out God?   Canst thou find out the Almighty unto perfection? It is as high as heaven; what canst thou do? deeper than Sheol; what canst thou know?" The words happen to be Zophar's, but any one of the speakers might have uttered them. And so we need not be surprised that the writer of the *Book of Job* does not even dream of attempting an analysis and elucidation of the problem before him such as might satisfy a western reader's mind.

And yet, in the end, *some* solution has evidently been arrived at, for Job's doubts are dispelled, and his murmurings at the divine dispensation are stilled. But that is not because the divine dispensation has ceased to be mysterious. Job is as far as ever from having any clear understanding of the perplexing providences seen in human lives, and if we use the phrase, "the solution of the problem," in speaking both of the *Republic* and of the *Book of Job*, it must be used in quite different senses.

Some have supposed that the real solution is to be looked for in the prologue, where Satan is permitted by God to afflict Job in order to prove his steadfast uprightness. These first chapters present a marked contrast to the rest of the book. They are in prose, not in poetry, and the scene is laid, not on earth, in the land of Uz, but in Heaven, "in the presence of the Lord." One thinks of Raphael's "Transfiguration," where two planes are seen, the heavenly and the earthly, and the upper, perhaps, supplies what the lower sphere has need of. But in all probability the prose prologue merely reproduces the original folk-tale of Job's fortunes, to which some later gifted thinker has added the tremendous poem of the controversy. Certainly the suggestion of the prologue that trials and sufferings may be tests of faithfulness, is, to our minds, no more an adequate and complete solution than the other suggestions made by the three friends and Elihu, that they are punishment for sin, or are warnings sent lest the righteous fall into sin through self-satisfied spiritual pride. There may be truth in each of these three suggestions, but they are not, either singly or collectively, the whole truth. And, in any case, Job himself knows nothing of what the prologue narrates, and his acquiescence at the end cannot by any possibility be ascribed to anything there revealed.

Clearly what has changed his attitude from complaints to trust can only be the series of speeches in which the Almighty Himself suddenly breaks His long silence and answers Job out of the whirlwind. But it is not at once apparent in what sense these speeches furnish an answer to Job's perplexities. For Job, while briefly commended as being nearer the truth than his friends, is nevertheless rebuked for seeking to penetrate the inscrutable mystery of God's ways and purposes. True, God, whose continued silence has been Job's greatest trial, now speaks to him, and even if it is in reproof, the mere fact that He does speak may have done something to quiet Job's perturbed heart. But far more it is the vision of the God of nature, so impressively revealed to him, that changes and transfigures him.

He has been eager to come face to face with God,

and, as in a court of law, plead his case with his adversary (for so he actually terms God Himself), full of confidence that he can meet any charge God might bring against him. But the God with whom he is now confronted wholly disregards the issue Job had wished to argue. He does not speak as an accusing adversary, nor even as the awful Judge of the hearts of men. Instead, He dwells upon all the manifestations that nature everywhere affords of the orderly care which He bestows upon this vast and manifold universe that His power has created and continues to direct and sustain. Job's complaint (as Professor McFadyen puts it) has been that "there is no moral order; there is not even an immoral order; there is simply no order at all," only caprice and confusion. He is shown that if the universe is a mystery, it is an orderly mystery, full of thought and concern and purpose. And Job, whose trouble was not an intellectual but a religious one, is content to bow his head in humble contrition and simple trust before the God revealed in nature—a revelation which, in all ages, and with all sorts and conditions of men, has won a response in the heart and conscience of mankind.

These are the words of Dean Bradley's summing up: "Those who tell us that the one great lesson of the whole book is to hold up the patriarch Job as the pattern of mere submission, mere resignation — or those who search for a [full explanation and final vindication] of God's mode of government—or those lastly who find in it a revelation of the sure and certain hope of a blessed immortality, can scarcely have studied Job's language. . . . One thought and one only is brought into the foreground. The world is full of mysteries, strange, unapproachable, overpowering mysteries that you cannot read. Trust, trust in the power and in the wisdom and in the goodness of Him, the Almighty one, who rules it."

Job's criticism in the earlier chapters is neither withdrawn nor modified; it is simply forgotten. His reasoning is not confuted, nor his understanding enlightened; but his heart is comforted and at peace. And the argument that has wrought the change is, in substance, the same that we find used in the Sermon on the Mount: "Wherefore if God so clothes the grass of the field, shall he not much more clothe you, O ye of little faith?"

This implied contrast of reasoning and faith as a pair of mutually exclusive and antagonistic opposites suggests an interesting point. It has been objected to Plato's reasoned argument that while he often stirs the heart as well as stimulates the brain, while he moves the reader to sympathy with all that is noble and true, while he powerfully appeals to all our ideals of right and duty, yet he does not really prove his point. The only answer to this is to ask: Is it possible for any one to prove the truths which are of highest import? At the back of all arguments about good and evil, right and wrong, all arguments involving ultimate values or the obligation of duty, we find something not capable of rational proof and demonstration, but depending on the response of the soul and conscience to something that must be accepted as an act of faith, unanalysable, and, while reasonable, yet not demonstrable. So it is in the last analysis also with what we call exact science. Underneath all scientific arguments and proofs lie certain assumptions, such as the conception of uniformity, law, and order in nature, or the validity of logical inferences; assumptions which, in reality, involve an act of faith.* So it is with Plato's argument; and so it is with the doctrines of the New Testament. The things that it would seem most important to have proved, in order that man might be sustained by absolute certainty, are precisely the things that cannot be either proved or disproved. Certainly the reader who has come under the spell of Plato's inspiring thought and magical style, whose eyes have been opened by him to new visions of truth and goodness and beauty, is not greatly disturbed by the objection that Plato has not proved his case, and does not care overmuch whether the process by which he reaches his conclusions be termed reason or faith.

One final point of comparison remains to be briefly dealt with. In the concluding verses of the *Book of*

* "The basis of science lies in a certain trust in nature—that nature will prove 'reasonable,' or will behave in such a way as corresponds with the demands of reason for a certain order or uniformity. It is obvious that this could not and cannot be proved. . . .

"The uniformity of nature never can become a self-evident proposition. It is a venture of faith—confirmed in experience, but not so confirmed that 'the future will resemble the past' can become anything more than an act of faith."—C. GORE.

Job, in the brief prose epilogue which corresponds to the much longer prose prologue, all Job's former prosperity is restored to him in full measure, sheep, oxen, camels, sons and daughters. To some, this reparation is a sad anticlimax; it seems a weak concession or reversion to the traditional Old Testament prudential philosophy, or even an admission that Satan was right after all when he asked: "Does Job serve God for naught?" But (as Froude points out) the really significant thing is that Job's prosperity is restored only when he has no need of it. Now that his heart is at rest, since he is sure of God, worldly prosperity and adversity are slight things by comparison; they are counted as the small dust of the balance.

Something very similar is to be found in the last book of the *Republic*. It will be remembered that, in order to study justice and injustice in and for themselves, extreme cases were assumed; the unjust man was given every possible advantage, in wealth and power and reputation and impunity, while the righteous man was in every respect the opposite. But now that it has been shown that, even so, with "Right for ever on the scaffold, Wrong for ever on the throne," yet justice is more choice-worthy than injustice, whatever befalls—now that this has been shown, Socrates asks that what he had conceded for the sake of argument be withdrawn; as he puts it: "Return to me what you borrowed in the discussion." For in reality, he holds, the facts of life are far otherwise than had been assumed. As a rule the just man does not miss the recompense he deserves, and the unscrupulous self-seeker fails, as a rule, to maintain his ill-gotten gains. He is like many a runner in a race, who starts out well, but has no staying powers.

Note the words *as a rule*. Plato does not hold that all is as it should be in this material and transitory state of things. There is far too much evidence of pain and suffering, of evil and frustration and imperfection in many forms, for him to accept the easy optimism of "God's in his heaven; all's right with the world" —at least, with this world. But the present life is not all, he believes, and in the world to come all these failures and inequities disappear, and there the gods dispense perfect justice to every man according as his life has been good or evil. "This then," says Socrates in summing up, "must be our conviction about the just man, that even if poverty or sickness or any other supposed evil do come upon him, all these things will in the end work together for good both in life and in death. For the gods assuredly never neglect the man who is eager to become righteous, and who seeks, by the practice of goodness, to grow into likeness to God, as far as that is possible for man."

And thus the just man of Plato's argument, like Job, has prosperity restored to him when it has been found that he does not need it for true felicity and well-being. And, in addition, Plato gives him what Job did not have to console and inspire him, the certain hope of a fuller and completer life beyond the grave.

The last words of the *Book of Job* are: "So Job died, being old and full of days." And that is the end of Job. Plato closes the *Republic* with these words: "Believing that the soul is undying, we shall hold ever to the upward way, and follow after righteousness and wisdom always, that . . . both here and in that other life it may be well with us."

CHRIST AND GREEK THOUGHT

NOT infrequently, and particularly at the season of Advent, one hears a sermon preached on the deplorable conditions prevailing in the Graeco-Roman world at the time of Christ's coming, and the marvellous changes due to his coming. Naturally the contrast will be all the more effective if the evils of that pagan world are painted in the blackest possible colours. If on the one side is put a lost mankind, as portrayed in the first chapter of Romans, and on the other side the ideals of the Sermon on the Mount, the contrast readily lends itself to some very vivid wordpainting and some very effective rhetoric. Whether, on reflection, an enlightened hearer would find such a sermon quite convincing is another question. It may occur to him, in the first place, to wonder whether the argument has been based on a thorough knowledge of all the facts and a quite candid survey of all the evidence. And it may, in the second place, appear to him that to recommend the Christian world as being superior to a very degraded type of civilization is scarcely the highest form of eulogy. Let me dwell for a few moments on these two objections before attempting to show a more excellent way of proving the preeminence of Christianity.

Undoubtedly in that ancient world, for all its culture, its magnificence, and its well-ordered stability, there was much that was desperately evil. But it was far from being wholly given over to uncleanness and decadence. A careful observer would find not a few grounds for thinking that the pure-minded Virgil was not wholly wrong in believing that a better day was dawning for mankind, and in dreaming of the return of a golden age to earth. Certainly we who have just emerged from the most awful war the world has known and are finding the problems it has left to us extremely hard to solve, are not justified by the security of our own glass-house in throwing stones at the age which, after a century of bitter and devastating civil war, was re-establishing a widespread and enduring peace that, for two centuries at least, gave to the civilized world better government and a happier existence than some parts of it have ever since known until our own day. The brighter side of the picture, so far as conditions in Rome and Italy are concerned, has been described in these words: "The wits and satirists of the period give us highly coloured pictures of the scandals and intrigues of the court, the vices, follies, and fashions of the smart set, and the vulgar display of the newly rich. But from other sources, less piquant and exciting to read, but certainly not less truthful, we learn of families, both humble and noble, which maintained the old Roman traditions of uprightness and devotion to duty, of women worthy of being ranked with the most honourable matrons of republican times, of men who used their wealth in the service of their fellow-men, of parents who trained their children according to wholesome ideals of clean living, and of numberless people in the common walks of life with honest, homely ideals and virtuous family affection, proud of their industries and sustaining one another by help and kindness. We learn from many sources of the frequent endowment of educational and charitable foundations, of orphanages and other private benefactions to relieve want and suffering. The quiet country districts of Italy especially remained, as they had always been, the home of an unspoiled and frugal race, kindly, industrious, and self-respecting, content with the common round of useful labour and simple pleasure."

But even if the picture were one of unrelieved gloom, it is doubtful whether this is either a fair or ultimately an effective kind of apologetic argument. It is an easy victory, and one scarcely worth the effort, that is gained by showing that the teachings of Jesus call for a far nobler and purer life than that lived by the people of His day, Roman or Greek or Jewish, pagan or Pharisee. So also do those teachings put to shame the nations of medieval Europe and those of modern Christendom. Our own Anglo-Saxon civilization of to-day could be shown to be far inferior to almost any other in the present or the past, if the same method were followed of contrasting the lamentable practice of the one with the admirable ideals of the other. One can easily imagine a Chinese Buddhist, for example, setting forth the humane, peace-loving, high-minded principles of his religion, and showing how superior they are to the crimes and civic corruption and moral profligacy of which the newspapers of

Christian North America are full. A juster method would be to compare ideals with ideals, and practice with practice. That might not lend itself so readily to pulpit eloquence, though for edification it should be no whit inferior; and it might demand a better knowledge of history than the training of ministers seems to aim at ensuring.

Here it may not be out of place to say, in passing, that it is surely an anomaly that theological courses of study, in this country at least, should lay so much stress on the history and development of the Semitic races, and so little on the history and development of the Graeco-Roman world. Yet the latter would seem to be as necessary for the comprehension of the New Testament as the former for Old Testament study, to say nothing of its immense importance in connection with the growth of the Christian Church and the development of Christian doctrine. It is as if, in order to understand the genius of Napoleon and the nature of his impact on the world, one were set to study everything bearing on Corsica and its people from prehistoric times, while giving very perfunctory attention to the conditions prevailing in France and Europe prior to his appearance on the scene. The parallel is not perfect at all points, to be sure; that Jesus was a Jew is of far greater consequence than that Napoleon was a Corsican. Still, so far as concerns the sphere of its influence, Christendom has meant Europe rather than Palestine, Egypt, or Babylonia. But all this is a digression from our proper subject.

Instead of contrasting Christ's preaching with pagan
practice, especially when this latter is represented at its
worst, it would seem to be a more profitable line of inquiry to ask what ideals we have in Christianity that
the world we call pagan did not have, even when taken
at its best. For we must always bear in mind that in
that ancient world were men of noble character and
high principles, whose profound insight into the great
problems of the nature of God and man have left a
deep impress on our moral and spiritual thinking. Is
it not worth while to ask: In just what respects did
Christ's teaching transcend the highest reach of these
greatest of thinkers? For if we can find the answer
to that question, we may be sure that there we have
put our finger upon truths of the most vital importance to mankind, nor would it be too much to say
that there we may expect to find the peculiar message
Jesus had for the world, the central and vital truths
He would have us learn and build our lives upon.
By approaching the ancient world in that spirit, we
may hope to be more effective apologists of our faith.
And, apart from that, seeing that so much of our
intellectual and spiritual equipment is inherited from
the Greeks, who are our ancestors after the spirit, it
is surely as important for us, as Christians, to discover
wherein Christ transcended Plato and the best Greek
thought as to know wherein He transcended Moses
and the prophets.

In three directions, it is here suggested, such a
superiority may be shown to exist. Each of the three
points deserves a far more elaborate and thorough

K

treatment than can here be attempted; but even the general outline that follows will, it is hoped, be sufficient to indicate clearly the nature and the importance of the difference discoverable under each head.

(1) First may be put the personality of God, if that most disputable term may be used to express the nature of a supreme being with whom, in some real and not merely magical sense, man can have communion, however incomprehensible and ineffable may be the essential nature of that being in all its fullness. The Greek, in his marvellously rich mythology, had an abundance of gods who were indisputably persons, in that they were little more than magnified human beings, combining superhuman powers with human frailties. These gods were not patterns of conduct even to those who prayed to them; human goodness had for the normal Greek other sanctions and other origins than the divine nature. But the great poets and thinkers of Greece, without, to be sure, wholly abandoning the traditional recognition of a plurality of gods made in man's image, yet also attained the far higher conception of a supreme God of righteousness as well as of power, a God whose attributes are worthy of man's reverence, and in assimilation to whose divine nature man's virtue and well-being consist.

The teaching of the Greek philosophers is naturally more definite and more profound than the occasional glimpses of the poets, whom we may, therefore, disregard, as we proceed to compare the God of Greece's greatest thinkers with the God whom Jesus sought to reveal to men. That there is in man something akin to the Divine, that he is "not an earthly, but a heavenly plant," is one of Plato's most assured beliefs and the chief inspiration of his idealism.   He teaches that man realizes himself and attains fullness of life by cultivating this divine element, which is the true man, and that our one aim should be to become as like God as possible, by which he means developing our powers of intellectual and spiritual insight to the utmost and keeping under control the impulses and appetites of our lower nature.   But with all Plato's moving and genuine fervour, his God is in effect an abstract principle, revealed in the order and rationality of the universe, a transcendent and supreme reality as impersonal and remote as Arnold's "power not ourselves that makes for righteousness."   So far removed is this supreme reality in its absolute perfection from man and his world that the Platonists came in the end to postulate intermediate divine beings in order to bring the ultimate reality and our sensible existence into some conceivable relation.   Aristotle's conception of the great First Cause is even more abstract and absolute than Plato's, and correspondingly more removed from all contact with our imperfect nature.   Aristotle's God is too perfect to be a moral being, for morality involves the possession of a lower nature, to be brought into subjection to a higher; and his God is too perfect to be either the creator or the providential ruler of anything so imperfect as a material and changing universe.   Dwelling in perfect bliss, in a timeless eternity of self-contemplation (for even to be conscious of anything less perfect than Himself would detract from His absolute perfection), God is not concerned with this world or with mankind. And yet, according to Aristotle, these depend on God, being moved and drawn by the attraction of His perfection, and in that upward aspiration they find such measure of perfection and satisfaction as is possible for them. It is a significant fact that in proportion as the Greek conception of God became more lofty and more absolute in its perfection, it became less and less personal. In dealing with such a God there might be harmony and imitation and dependence, but these are not synonymous with communion and fellowship.

The Christian conception of God, while in no way inferior to the Greek in regard to His purity, righteousness, power, and absolute perfection, is completely different in the importance attached to the fatherhood of God. Nothing is more fundamental in the experience and the teaching of Jesus than His belief that God is His Father; nor does His own unique sense of sonship exclude our sonship also; one and the same being is "my Father and your Father." His parables and conversations are full of a Heavenly Father who knows us and cares for us, not collectively or in the mass as mankind, but for each one of us individually; who seeks us out even when we have forgotten Him, and who welcomes and rejoices in our fullest trust in Him. The truest way to think of God, He teaches, is to think of Him as our Father, and as a Father also who is so truly a person that we can best come to understand Him by coming to know Jesus himself, the express image of a Christlike God. Of the perfection of God Jesus has no doubt, but it is a perfection in which His children are invited to partake (Matt. v. 48), and it is expressed, not by emphasizing the gulf created by His eternal majesty, His unsearchable wisdom, and His awful holiness, but by the argument based on human fatherhood and "How much more shall your Father which is in heaven!"

(2) Closely connected with this belief in the fatherhood of God is the emphasis laid on self-sacrificing love as a primary attribute of God himself and as the highest conceivable motive in human relations. Not that such love was unknown to Greek experience. Ever since there were mothers it must have abounded in human lives, and many a story in Greek legend and history tells of a readiness to sacrifice one's all unselfishly for the sake of others. But it is a noteworthy fact that self-sacrificing love was not consciously recognized as existing; no word or common phrase in Greek expresses it; nor does it find any place in the most acute analysis of human motives in Greek writers. What seems to us like unselfish patriotism was explained and justified as far-sighted self-regard; a man's welfare, it was argued, is so dependent on his country's freedom, that in serving it even unto death he is but working for his own best interests. Aristotle's "true friendship" is really based on the principle of *quid pro quo*. This, the highest and rarest of all types of friendship, according to him, is friendship between the best of men who mutually bless each other with their goodness; and it is rare simply because such men are rare, and more rarely still are intimates.

In another passage, Aristotle does recognize that it is the mark of a good man to take less than his rightful due in favour of others. But so far is this from the love that seeketh not her own that he goes on to suggest that perhaps in return for this abatement of his rights the good man is securing for himself some other good thing, such as winning the esteem of others or attaining self-perfection.

A university sermon preached a few years ago in Convocation Hall raised a question which Plato also faces in the famous apologue of the Cave in the *Republic*, and curiously, the Christian preacher had no other answer to give than Plato's; in fact, his whole line of reasoning, while apparently owing nothing to Plato, might be found in the *Republic*. The text was: "We that are strong ought to bear the infirmities of the weak," and the preacher undertook to answer the question: "Why should we?" In Plato's apologue, those who have been set free from the shadow life of the cave, and have learned to understand and enjoy the real world above, are sent back into the gloom to give what help and enlightenment they can to their fellows still in bondage there; and the question is put to Socrates, whether it is not unjust to ask men who might have continued to live a more complete and perfect life to sacrifice it in order to help others. The answer he gives is, in effect: "That depends on whether (through a co-operative organization of society as in the *Republic*) those still in the cave had contributed to give these men their chance to escape from it. If they had, then the sacrifice is but the honest repayment of a debt." Otherwise, it is implied, such a sacrifice has no justification. The only important difference in the university preacher's answer was that the debt which the strong ought to repay is one owed, not only to the rest of the community, but to God, from whom we have received so much.

But is this the real answer of Christianity? What debt of Christ's was He repaying, and to whom, when for us men and for our salvation He took upon Him our flesh and suffered death upon the Cross? The New Testament writers are never tired of dwelling on the revelation of overflowing love, both the Father's and the Son's, which we have in the Incarnation and the Cross. And all down the ages ever since, the recognition of this love has kindled in innumerable hearts a similar love, utterly forgetful of self, thinking of no reward, but rejoicing in service that it needs no sense of debt or duty to inspire. So Paul prayed that it might be: "Let this mind be in you which was also in Christ Jesus, who, though being in the form of God, emptied himself, taking the form of a servant, and humbled himself, becoming obedient unto death." Unselfish love, springing from the natural heart of man, may often have been witnessed before Jesus came, but its import had been unperceived even by the keenest minds of Greece. Now it was so amazingly manifested that all the world could see it for what it is, and the most ignorant of men could talk of it with an understanding, as well as a grateful, heart.

The noble, but still essentially self-regarding, question, "What shall I do to inherit eternal life?" a Greek

like Plato could, and did, ask; but of that other
and higher self-forgetting motive, which breathes the
very spirit of Christ, Greek thought remained quite
unconscious.

(3) The last point of difference to be noted has far
more significance than might at first appear, and concerns the relative value of the various powers and
capacities of man. The Greek regarded it as axiomatic that reason is the essential thing in man, and, as
Aristotle says, *is* man. Men rise or fall in the scale
according to the strength and development of their
reasoning powers. To Plato and Aristotle, the man
likest to God, the one in whom the divine element in
man is at its highest, is the man possessed of the
supremest powers of intellectual and spiritual * insight, and "divine philosophy" is the human activity
that most nearly resembles what they conceive to be
the activity of the supreme being, God. In Plato's
view, we might say, man's soul has but one window
through which it can see God and through which the
light of divine truth can enter, and that window is
named Philosophy. He may have conceived of the
final vision of the supreme good as achieved directly
and not through processes of reasoning, but none the
less it is only by a long and arduous course of intellectual discipline and philosophical thinking that the
stage is reached where this direct vision become possible.

* The word "spiritual" is added lest it be thought that the wisdom
so valued by the Greek meant mere brain power or mental alertness
or accumulated learning; as Emerson says, "in Plato, intellect is
always moral." On the other hand spiritual insight was not divorced
from, nor distinguished from, the capacity for abstract reasoning.

There are, in truth, no beatitudes in Greek writings for the poor in intellectual ability. Plato would agree that it is hard for the rich man to enter the Kingdom of Heaven; but for the common man, untrained in logical processes, and incapable of abstract reasoning, he would think it, not hard, but quite impossible. All the schools of thought which derive from Socrates define virtue in terms of knowledge, and they all make a sharp distinction between those who are possessed of wisdom and endowed with intellectual power and those who are not. Only the former live the true life of man; only they attain true felicity; only they enjoy the smile of Heaven's blessing. The one partial exception is the Epicurean school, which prided itself on having a doctrine that required no exceptional intellect to understand it, and which owed to that fact no small part of such popularity as it enjoyed. Similarly, the rapid spread of Christianity was due largely to the universal invitation it extended: "Whosoever will, let him take the water of life freely." No exceptional mental equipment was needed to understand the fatherhood of God and the love of Jesus; and the new gospel appealed particularly to those for whom the best Greek thought had no message and held out no hope, the common folk, the weak and the broken-hearted, those who labour and are heavy-laden, whether bond or free. It is the crowning glory of Christianity that it opens wide the door of hope to all, for all are capable of love and trust and obedience, and it is these, and not philosophic insight, that give entrance to the Kingdom of God proclaimed by Jesus.

A Greek might have understood a mission to extend
to the Brahmins our superior enlightenment (even if
it would not occur to him to send one), but he could
never have dreamed of offering eternal life to the "un-
touchables." And had it been a Greek who wrote
the story of the conversations which Jesus had with
Nicodemus and the woman of Samaria, it would not
have been to the ignorant, uncomprehending woman,
but to the educated ruler, that the great truth would
have been imparted of the well of water springing up
into everlasting life; as it would not have been the
respectable Pharisee, but the Samaritan of questionable
character, that would have been warned of the necessity of a complete regeneration. With good reason
may all the world join with Jesus in thanking the
Father because things that have been hidden from the
wise and prudent have been revealed unto babes.

In these three particulars, then, we seem to have
found truths which are cardinal points in Christ's
teaching, but to which the best and noblest Greek
thought had not attained; and all three would seem to
be embraced in the great evangelical text: "God so
loved the world that he gave his only begotten Son,
that whosoever believeth in him should not perish
but have eternal life." John 3:16

THE GROWTH OF LEGENDS

PILATE's query, "What is truth?" implies, of course, that with equal justification one might put the question, "What is untruth?" And if truth eludes precise definition, untruth is equally hard to delimit, so varied are the myriad forms that it may assume. To certain of these forms the terms *mythical*, *fabulous*, *legendary*, *fictitious*, are all applied, often without much discrimination. Yet distinctions may be made, and the careful writer does not treat these words as quite interchangeable. For our present purpose it will be sufficient to distinguish between the two words *myth* and *legend*, and thus fix more definitely the subject of these pages.

The distinction would seem to be this: the myth, properly speaking, deals with the supernatural, with the explanation of the origin of the universe or of some part of it; the legend narrates the doings of mankind. The myth is concerned with that which lies before and beyond history; the legend purports to be history. A theory, once sufficiently current to have a name, Euhemerism, held that the divine beings of the myths were after all only exceptional human beings, men whose great deeds had been magnified by excessive hero-worship until, in time, they took on superhuman proportions; in effect, that myths are but the development or the extension of legends. Whatever truth this explanation may have in isolated cases here and there, it has long been discarded as an adequate account of the origin of mythology in general.

Both myth and legend, again, have a relation to religion, but not the same relation. Many systems of religion, especially those which we call pagan, consist chiefly of myth and magic, the myth often arising out of magic, that is, out of the desire to give some explanation of a magical rite or taboo. On the other hand, the relation of the legend to religion is a quite casual one, as may be seen if we turn to the origin of the word and trace the development of its meaning. The Latin word *legenda*, meaning "things worth reading," was applied in medieval times to accounts of the life-story of some saint or of some particular miraculous incident in the life of a saint. One notable example of this earlier meaning is found in the so-called *Golden Legend*, a famous collection of lives of the saints of the Church, which was written in the thirteenth century and became the great textbook of legendary lore in the Middle Ages. From this original connection with edifying biography, the term was extended to include any marvellous or extraordinary narrative handed down by tradition, without any of the original restrictions to the miraculous doings or experiences of Christian saints and without any association with religious practice or belief.

The connection of legend with history is much closer and much more important than the connection of legend with myth. To the believer in a legend, of course, the difference between that legend and history does not exist. And we also, without committing ourselves to the cynical definition of history as "what men have agreed to believe," may admit that legendary and unhistorical are not completely convertible and synonymous terms. The legendary is not necessarily wholly false, any more than history is necessarily wholly true. For legends may, and often do, contain a considerable element of historic truth, but usually with distortions and accretions due to the weakness of men's memory and the strength of their imagination.

Two legends of our own times may serve to illustrate some of the characteristics of the class. Early in the Great War two stories gained wide currency, and one of them is probably still accepted as true by thousands of people. This latter, the story of angels intervening at Mons between the Germans and the hard-pressed British, might seem to be more properly termed a myth, as introducing the element of the supernatural. But it gained credence as a piece of sober history, to the truth of which many were said to be ready to bear witness, and so the story may be held to be more properly called a legend. In truth, it lies in the debatable ground between the two, and its origin was partly in the imagination of a writer who aimed at nothing more than an effective piece of imaginative fiction, and partly in the overwrought state of mind of people at that time. It was the joint offspring of the literary art and abnormal psychology. The other story told how Russian battalions brought from Archangel to the north of Scotland were then transported secretly at night by rail to the Channel ports and thence to France. This story was widely believed, until more accurate knowledge of the forces fighting in France showed that it was pure fiction, although it has since been made known that some such project was actually at one time suggested to the War Office. The accepted explanation of the origin of this story is that at some junction point in England, one night, a railway porter saw a train of carriages filled with Highland recruits on their way south, and overheard these obviously un-English-looking people talking to one another in unintelligible Gaelic.

This last story, except for its lack of enduring vitality, might be taken as a good example of the legend according to its present-day meaning, which, as given in the *Encyclopaedia Britannica*, is "a story handed down without any foundation in history, but popularly believed to be true." In this definition, however, one phrase is altogether too sweeping: "without any foundation in history." The historical foundation in some legends may be very slight or wholly negligible; but in other cases there would seem to be a very considerable and a very important underlying basis of truth. The legend shades off into history by imperceptible degrees, and with the growth of knowledge or the shift of opinion, the legend of to-day may become the history of to-morrow, or the reverse process may take place.

In fact, apart from the wonderful achievements of natural and physical science in our day, it is doubtful if any aspect of the advance of knowledge made within the last generation is more notable than the rehabilitation of the legends that have come down to us from the past ages of the world, especially those dealing, or purporting to deal, with the beginnings of the Semitic and of the Graeco-Roman peoples. Legends that a generation ago were commonly regarded by the enlightened critic as wholly fabulous, figments of the imagination belonging to the childhood of our race, are no longer treated as purely fanciful and fictitious, but are recognized as very possibly embodying the records of long-distant events, not written with ink, nor inscribed on stone, but stored in men's hearts and memories; records which, in the lapse of long years, were doubtless often altered in strange ways, but which may still have retained some valuable remnant of their original contents. In days when writing was either non-existent or a rare accomplishment, and when the human memory was necessarily, therefore, more exercised and more depended upon; in days when generation after generation of men lived more continuously in one locality than is ever done in our restless modern times; in such circumstances oral tradition might be transmitted for unbelievably long periods, without more contamination of the truth than may repeatedly be found in the written accounts of contemporary events by uncritical recorders or in the newspaper reports of yesterday's happenings.

In part, this change of attitude to the legends of antiquity is due to the decipherment of ancient records, like the Egyptian hieroglyphics and the cuneiform tablets, which have added enormously to the ancient historical documents in existence with which to compare and test the legends that have survived. And, in part, the change is due to the work of the archaeologists, whose discoveries have added, not centuries, but millenniums to the ages of which we may now consider ourselves as possessing some trustworthy historical knowledge. No small part of this increased knowledge of man's remote past comes from the new value now attached to ancient legends, as being in some sense historical documents, without thereby losing any of their value as stories that have delighted mankind for ages.

In instance after instance the archaeologist has discovered something that goes to confirm the stories of Homer and Herodotus, as well as of the Biblical narrative; not in all their details, of course, but in some important point which shows that these stories were more than the pure product of the storyteller's imagination. And in instance after instance the deciphered hieroglyphic or cuneiform inscription has corroborated the statements or justified the implications of old-world legendary traditions to which scholars had attached no weight. The most recent example is furnished by the exploration of the site of Ur of the Chaldees, where Woolley and his associates have found apparently indisputable evidence of the destruction of the city and its civilization, at an early period of its history, by a flood of such magnitude as would quite account for the widespread tradition among many ancient peoples of just such a calamity.

The outstanding example of this complete change of opinion is in connection with the early history of the

countries about the Aegean. The Greek histories
that were the recognized authorities sixty years ago
either did not deign to refer at all to the rich store of
legends possessed by the Greeks, or treated them as
in no sense historical. The very existence of Homer's
Troy and the Trojan War was regarded as open to
grave question; while the stories of Perseus and
Andromeda, of Jason and the Argonauts, of Theseus
and the Minotaur, and the like, were classed, so far
as credibility goes, with the tales of Sindbad and Jack
the Giant-killer. Yet at that very time Henry Schliemann was unearthing the ruins of Troy, nay, of a
succession of Troys, built on the same site in succes-
sive ages, and two of them obviously destroyed by
capture and fire; and the same Schliemann was shortly
after to open up the marvellous treasure-house of the
royal graves at Mycenae. These he mistakenly, but
not unnaturally, thought to be the burial-places of
King Agamemnon and his household, but they have
since been proved to antedate the Trojan War by
several centuries. Similarly, later investigation revealed that, of the two burnt cities, the one to be
identified with Homer's Troy is not the earlier, or
second, as Schliemann thought, but the much later or
sixth city. Thus the archaeologist and his spade have
not only shown that there was more than the critical
historian had supposed in Homer's tales of battles
fought on the ringing plains of windy Troy; they
have also uncovered evidence of those brave men
that, all unsung, lived, as Horace tells us, long before
Agamemnon.

L

As the last quarter of the nineteenth century in this way extended by four or five hundred years the period for which we have at least some knowledge of the Aegean world, so the later discoveries of Sir Arthur Evans in Crete during the first quarter of this century have added still another thousand years or more of which some real knowledge is possessed. However, until the Cretan script can be deciphered, what is known does not include as yet any detailed events or the knowledge of any individual persons or their doings, but consists chiefly of the light thrown on the growth and development of material civilization in the Bronze Age, and on the movements of races and the contacts with other lands about the eastern Mediterranean.

It is now, for instance, matter of sober history that during the time that the house of Pelops reigned in Mycenae the Aegean world was in a state of ferment, and that tribes mentioned in contemporary inscriptions and records, and identified with those whom we know as Achaeans, Danai, Lydians, Mysians, Sardinians, Etruscans, and Philistines, sailed southward out of Asia Minor and the Aegean islands, and raided Egypt and its adjacent dependencies, much as the Northmen, more than two thousand years afterwards, raided France and Britain. A close parallel to the settlement of the Northmen in Normandy is to be found in the settlement of the once mysterious Philistines, about 1200 B.C., on the coast of what was later known as Palestine, and also in the occupation in the far west of Etruria and Sardinia by others of these raiders.   In this connection it should be noted that the ancient world always retained the tradition that the Etruscans had come originally from Asia Minor, a tradition which is now supported by documentary evidence.

The changed attitude of present-day historians is exemplified in the monumental *Cambridge Ancient History*, now being published, which embodies the work of many of the most eminent of English-speaking historians and archaeologists.   The general editor of this work, Professor Bury, the Cambridge Professor of Ancient History, in a chapter dealing with the so-called Heroic Age of Greece, writes thus: "It has been common in modern times to regard these and the other heroes of this age, whose names come into the fairy - tales, as purely mythical creations. The later Greeks, in criticizing the records of their past, had no doubt that they were historical persons who actually ruled in Argos and other kingdoms; and, after a period of extreme scepticism, many modern critics have begun to revert to the Greek view as that which explains the evidence most satisfactorily and simply.   It has been adopted in this chapter without hesitation.   The heroes of these tales, like the geographical scenes in which they moved, were real, and there was always something in the events of their lives that provided a motive for the legends which were woven round them."

How different from this was the scepticism current half a century ago may be shown by a quotation from Adolph Holm, whose well-balanced *History of Greece* is still one of the sanest and best we have. After a detailed examination of the stories connected with Minos, Holm pronounces this judgment: "Minos is a mythical personage, like Perseus and Heracles, and the actions which are ascribed to him as history are nothing but a gradual accretion of legendary embellishments. . . . It would be easy to criticize other legends and show that even if they could have been founded on facts, there is not the slightest probability that such was the case." The historians of Holm's generation never dreamed that, before the first quarter of this century was ended, it would be the widely accepted view that the Greek traditional dates of the Trojan War and other legendary events are in general agreement with well-established results of archaeological research and Egyptian chronology, or that, from a comparison of these sources, the sober and authoritative *Cambridge Ancient History* would go so far as to date (approximately): "Cecrops between 1582 and 1556 B.C., Cadmus to 1313, Danaus to 1466, Pelops to 1283, Minos to 1229, while the Trojan War may probably be dated to 1192–83, and about 1104 the great Dorian invasion, which really marks the end of the prehistoric age and of the marvellous Bronze-Age civilization of Greece."

But if the scholars of half a century ago were too incredulous of these ancient stories having any value whatever beyond that of a fairy-tale, it would be as great an error to-day to be too ready to assume the credibility of a given legend, or too hasty in drawing inferences from its details. Each several case pre-

sents a distinct problem; each must be examined by
itself, and the most rigid tests must be applied before
even a probable conclusion can be safely drawn.
Naturally, therefore, no laws or principles of interpretation, no canons of criticism, can be enunciated
except the vaguest and most general. The distortions
and accretions which may at any stage result from the
play of imagination, from tribal prejudice or pride of
ancestry, from lapses of memory, or from purely
accidental and capricious causes, are infinite in variety
and unpredictable in their range. For these legends
are the offspring of the spirit of man; and this, like
the Divine Spirit of which it is born, is as the wind
that bloweth where it listeth. Of a living legend also
it may be said: "Thou hearest the sound thereof, but
canst not tell whence it cometh and whither it goeth."

Instead, therefore, of attempting to treat the growth
of legends as if it were the subject-matter of an exact
science which can be reduced to system, with general
laws and principles of uniform and precise application,
I shall follow the pleasanter and, perhaps, not less
profitable course of illustrating how legends change
and grow. For this purpose, a legend long current
in Provence will serve admirably, a legend which may
be found set forth in more or less detail in many books
of travel dealing with that part of France. This story,
for one thing, illustrates nearly every kind of thing
that could possibly happen to a legend in the course
of its development; and there is this further inestimable advantage that, instead of having, as is usual,
to infer the historical from the legendary, we have

quite definite knowledge of the events out of which the legend arose, and can thus follow with fuller appreciation its various changes. It will be well to begin with the historical foundation, and then survey the fantastic structure that later ages have built upon it.

About 115 B.C., rumours began to reach Rome of a great movement of Germanic tribes coming from the far north towards Italy. Nearly three centuries had elapsed since the capture and sacking of Rome by the Gauls under Brennus, in 390 B.C., an event which had remained ever after in the memories of the Romans as the greatest disaster of their history. And yet, after all, it was but a sudden raid by a swiftly moving band of rovers, who unexpectedly appeared, and then, their purpose accomplished, completely and at once disappeared from the scene. But in this later instance, an immense multitude of barbarians hovered for years about the borders of the Roman domain, defying every attempt to disperse them, defeating with heavy loss every Roman force that opposed them, and continually growing in numbers by the addition of other tribes as formidable as the original body.

This original tribe, the Cimbri, first approached Italy on the north-east frontier of the Alps, near the modern Carinthia. They defeated a Roman general who had treacherously and foolishly attacked them; then, instead of pressing forward into Italy, as might have been expected, they moved westwards, through Tyrol and Switzerland, into France, in the south-eastern part of which was the Roman province of Transalpine Gaul. Here again, they defeated more than one Roman general who sought to guard the province from invasion. Their laſt victory was also the completeſt. In 105 B.C., at Arausio (now Orange) on the Rhône, they utterly annihilated the combined armies of two of the best Roman generals. We are told that eighty thousand legionaries were killed, and half as many more camp-followers, and that but a bare handful escaped alive. For it was one cause of the terror inspired by these invaders that after a victory they slew all their prisoners. The defeat inflicted by Hannibal at Cannae, a century before, was always accounted the black day of Roman warfare; but the carnage at Arausio was even greater than at Cannae. No new army was ready to take the field, and, had the Cimbri chosen to march into Italy, there was absolutely nothing to hinder them. The panic among the residents of the Gallic Province was even greater than that which prevailed in Italy, and naturally so. They had the invaders at their doors; they had seen the wildness and ferocity of their appearance; they had heard the frenzied cries by which the Cimbrian women incited their men to battle; they knew how ruthless they were in the hour of victory; and it is not surprising that thousands of the provincials fled from their homes and took refuge in the wild recesses of their country.

An invasion of Italy by these hordes might have changed the whole course of European hiſtory; but Rome's good fortune intervened, and for some freakish reason the Cimbri went off into Spain for two years, during which time the great Roman general, Marius, was sent into Gaul, and there had time to develop the plans his military genius suggested for saving Italy. Meanwhile, the Cimbri had made little headway in attacking the warlike Celtiberians of northern Spain, and, tiring of this unprofitable warfare, they returned to Gaul. Here they marched steadily northwards, pillaging and terrorizing every district they traversed. But when they drew near the Channel, they found the resistance of the Belgic tribes as stubborn as that of the Celtiberians, and so they turned south again to resume their long-deferred march into Italy. By this time they had been joined by the Teutons and other Germanic tribes, and were vastly more formidable than when they first approached the Roman borders. Their numbers were well over a million, of whom three hundred and fifty thousand were fighting men.

And now Rome met with another piece of sheer good luck. The invading hosts divided; the Cimbri decided to go back through Switzerland to the pass by which they might easily have entered Italy eleven years before, while the Teutons and Ambrons were to cross the lower Rhône, march through the Province, and enter Italy by the western Alps. By this time, Marius had organized and disciplined his army, and had matured his plans for coping with the enemy.

To understand fully what happened, one should have a good contour map of the district before him; but a verbal description may indicate the essential features. For many leagues on each side of the mouth of the Rhône are wide tracts of low-lying lands, built up by the deposits of the river and broken everywhere by marshes, lagoons, and water-courses; a district quite

impassable, in those days, by any large body of people.
Between this fen district and the mountains that fill
the greater part of south-eastern France and culminate
in the Alps, is a tract of country with many hills and
low ridges, broken by wild gorges and precipitous
limestone cliffs.   So restricted were the practicable
routes through this part of Gaul two thousand years
ago, that Marius could be fairly certain where the
invaders would cross the Rhône, and knew that from
that point, one or other of two routes must be taken
to Italy.   This fact determined his strategy.   He made
his permanent camp in an impregnable entrenchment
a few miles east of the Rhône, and here he prepared
his men for the coming contest, and waited for the
enemy.   Finally they crossed the river where he had
expected, and for three days made fierce assaults on
his fortified camp that were repelled with heavy loss.
Then, as the Romans watched them, the Teuton hosts
slowly and interminably marched past the Roman lines
with jeers and taunts, and, after they had passed,
Marius, with his army, followed on their track.   He
withheld his men from attacking the main body until
they should be accustomed to the wild appearance and
savage cries of the Teutons; above all, he was waiting
for the occasion on which he had calculated.   He did,
however, embrace the opportunity that suddenly one
day presented itself of badly defeating an isolated body
of the invaders whom he caught at a disadvantage,
thus at once enraging the enemy and heartening his
own troops. Finally, some sixty miles from the
Rhône crossing, the Teutons reached a well-watered

plain near Aquae Sextiae (the modern Aix), a plain
overlooked from both north and south by ranges of
high hills; and now Marius judged the time was ripe
for the battle he had planned.

The victory he won was, in part, the victory of discipline and order over the reckless enthusiasm of
superior, but untrained, numbers. But it was also a
victory due to shrewd generalship and skilful handling
of forces. Marius posted his men on higher ground,
where the enemy, wild to avenge the resented slaughter
of their comrades a few days before, and contemptuous
of the Romans whom the Cimbri had so often defeated,
did not hesitate to climb, in stifling summer heat, in
order to attack the waiting Romans. At the same
time Marius had sent a force secretly by a circuitous
route to get among the hills on the opposite side of
the plain, and these, appearing in the enemy's rear at
a critical moment, completed their discomfiture.

The slaughter was tremendous; one hundred thousand were killed on the field of battle, and three hundred thousand women, children, and camp-followers
were either killed or made captives and slaves. The
danger that for a decade had threatened the inhabitants of the Province had, in a few hours, vanished
for ever. The wild barbarians, who had terrified them
as no modern people suffering an armed invasion can
well comprehend, were suddenly as if they had never
existed. A few words will complete the story. The
other division, the Cimbri, made its way into Italy,
and there Marius, having brought his victorious army
back, joined forces with the proconsul, Catulus, fell

upon the Cimbri at Vercellae, near Milan, and annihilated them as completely as he had the Teutons in
Gaul.   It was nearly four hundred years before barbarian invaders again set foot in Italy.

The circumstances of this invasion have been nar-
rated with such fullness for this reason, that only by
realizing the immensity of the terror that had hung
over the people of this region for years, and the com-
pleteness of their deliverance, can we understand the
deep impression the event made upon them, an impression so indelible that to this day the memory persists of the great victory.   Many local names help to
perpetuate the event.   In particular, overlooking the
battlefield is a bold height, rising three thousand feet
precipitously above the plain and known as Mont
Sainte-Victoire.   Note the word Sainte.   For some
years later, Julius Cæsar, the nephew of Marius,
dedicated a shrine in memory of the victory to his
patron goddess, Venus.   This, like many another
Roman temple, in time became a Christian shrine,
which was dedicated to a new saint, Saint Victory.
Still later, a monastery was built there on the heights,
the monastery of Sainte-Victoire.

Every spring, generation after generation, a procession made its way to this shrine, celebrating the ancient
but never-forgotten victory, and this custom was kept
up all through the centuries until the time of the
French Revolution.   When the procession reached
the summit, a bonfire was lighted, and round it the
peasants, adorned with garlands, would dance, shouting: "Victoire!   Victoire!"   The return was made late

at night, with the waving of boughs and with much
shouting. Next morning a mass was said at a little
village near by, on the route followed by the troops
sent by Marius to take the Teutons in the rear.
Finally the celebrants visited a wild chasm or abyss
among the rocks, down which the Romans had hurled
a hundred prisoners after the battle to propitiate the
nether powers. The traditional music to which the
annual procession marched to Mont Sainte-Victoire
was written down by a local priest before the ceremonies were discontinued, and is preserved for us
in certain of the books dealing with the history of
Provence. But though the ceremonies came to an
end amid the turmoil of the Revolution, the local
traditions connected with the victory of Marius still
persist with undiminished vitality.

So far, the story told at such length does not differ
essentially from scores of others which are on record,
where local tradition has retained for centuries some
fairly accurate memory of events which are also often
perpetuated in local place-names. The most singular
and interesting part of the story has still to be told, as
we trace the changes brought about in the original
form of the legend by time and accident and other
causes. It is these variations and accretions that so
admirably illustrate the development of legends in
general.

In Plutarch's *Life of Marius* we read how the soldiers
murmured at being restrained from battle with the
Teutons, and how Marius, who was secretly delighted
by their eagerness, sought to quiet them, assuring

them of his confidence in them, and disclosing that it was because of certain oracles that he was waiting for the right time and place for victory. "And in fact," continues Plutarch, "he used to take about with him, carried in state in a litter, a certain Syrian woman . . . who was said to be a prophetess, and he would offer sacrifices at her direction. She had sought an audience with the Roman Senate and had offered to foretell coming events, but had been rebuffed. Afterwards she got access to the women and gave them proofs of her gift, and in particular, sitting at the feet of Marius' wife during a gladiatorial fight, she had successfully predicted which one would be victorious. This led to her being sent to Marius by his wife, and by him she was shown much respect"; though Plutarch goes on to suggest that Marius merely pretended to share his wife's belief in the Syrian, whose reputation he shrewdly used to further his own designs.

This Syrian prophetess, then, was an important personage in the Roman army in the Province, and a relic of those days still existing there bears witness to this fact. Near Le Baux, a short distance from the permanent camp of Marius, where he trained his army while he waited for the return of the Germanic hosts, there is a white limestone hillside on which are carved three life-sized figures in a rectangular niche. The head and shoulders alone appear in the carving, and the three figures represent Marius, his wife Julia (who was the sister of Julius Cæsar's father), and, between them, the prophetess. Locally, the group is known as "Trémaïe." This name was originally Tres Marii, "the three of Marius's household." As we shall see, a very different interpretation is now put upon this name by the people of Provence.

Having spent so much time over the events of the ten or twelve years of the Germanic invasion, let me now make amends by summarizing in a single sentence the changes which the next ten or twelve centuries brought about. The memory of the battle still remained fresh in the people's minds, but, meanwhile, Christianity had been introduced into the Province, and in course of time it came to be understood that the three figures of the Trémaïé were those of the Biblical family of Bethany, Mary, Martha, and their brother Lazarus. How had so singular a change been brought about?

There was an early tradition current in Provence that, after the Crucifixion, these three friends of our Lord were set adrift by their enemies in Palestine, and that their boat was miraculously preserved from harm and brought to shore some miles east of the Rhône and south of Le Baux where the three figures are carved. The universal belief in Provence is that Christianity came to it, not by the usual channels, through the visits of missionaries of the Cross or the settling of converts in the district, but by refugees from the Holy Land who were among the closest friends of the Master. One is reminded of the story of Joseph of Arimathea being the first to bring Christianity to England at Glastonbury. This legend of Provence may, of course, have some basis or other in fact; of that there would seem to be neither proof nor disproof. Many of the details, however, are obviously not authentic, and some of them are clearly due to the Marius tradition. For example, there is a medieval legend that tells how Martha freed the people of Tarascon, on the lower Rhône, from the visitations of a monstrous dragon, and until as recently as 1904 there was annually enacted at Tarascon a dramatized pageant of Martha's victory over the Tarasque, as the dragon is called. It is a quite reasonable inference that all this is a reminiscence of the dread peril from which Marius delivered the Province.

But we have something better than merely conjecture and reasonable inference when we seek to trace the cause of the transformation of Marius and the two women, his wife and the prophetess, into the family of Bethany. Most readers have probably already suspected that the resemblance of the two names, Marius and Mary (or *Marium* and *Mariam* in the Latin forms from which the medieval and modern names would have been taken), had not a little to do with the confusion. But there is more than that. In the extract from Plutarch just quoted, two words were purposely omitted, which tell us that the Syrian prophetess was "named Martha." As she came from Syria, there is nothing surprising in her bearing that Semitic name. But what a remarkable coincidence it is! Here are two groups, each of three people, two women and a man, and two of each group bear practically identical names which figure in the two best-known traditions of that country. After the simple, unlettered peasantry were converted to Christianity and came to know something of the gospel story, the tendency to change the ascription from Marius, Martha, and Julia to Mary, Martha, and Lazarus must have been irresistible.* Marius's wife Julia had a most insignificant part in the story, and her very name had probably long been forgotten. The countryfolk knew of Julius Cæsar, the great conqueror of Gaul, but there was nothing to keep alive the memory of his aunt Julia, the wife of Marius.

In the rudely sculptured group of the three figures (probably carved by some of Marius's soldiers in their leisure hours, out of compliment to their general or respect for the prophetess), the central figure, Martha, has a peculiar headdress, a sort of eastern tiara, and a headdress of this kind persists on all the local representations in Provence of Saint Martha. Again, the figure of Marius has some marks of a consul's dress, and has short hair and a short beard. He, of course, has become Lazarus; and locally Saint Lazare is regularly portrayed with short hair and a short beard, instead of being given the flowing beard and hair usually attributed to Jews. The remaining figure, Julia, wearing the stole of a Roman matron, has become Mary; and thus, fantastic though it sounds, in this corner of France one finds a quite traceable connection between Mary of Bethany and Cæsar's aunt Julia.

This is by no means the end of the story. Traditions and legends that are not embalmed in books, but live

* It is, indeed, quite possible that the whole legend of the coming of the family of Bethany grew up out of this similarity of names.

only in men's memories, and are transmitted by word of mouth, are like gossip and scandal, in that they are continually growing and changing. The confusion and transformation just described were completed more than a thousand years ago. In the intervening centuries further complications have arisen, and various new elements have come into the legend. Of these, three in particular may be distinguished, each of them resulting in some further modification of the story associated with the Trémaïé.

All over Europe, in the replacing of pagan cults by Christianity, nothing is commoner than the retention of some ancient temple transformed into a Christian place of worship (as we have seen was done with the shrine on Mont Sainte-Victoire), or the incorporation of some pagan rite or festival, often with little change, except perhaps of name, into usages associated with the new Christian faith (as some of the revelries of the Roman Saturnalia live on in our Christmas festivities, held at the same time of the year). Now, on the coast of Provence, west of the mouth of the Rhône, was an ancient temple sacred to Venus, the sailor's patron goddess. This was easily and naturally changed to a church dedicated to the Virgin, Sainte Marie de la mer. In process of time, in ways of which no record exists, it came about that the point of arrival of the vessel from Palestine was transferred from the coast east of the Rhône mouth to this better-known seaport to the west, where was this shrine dedicated to Sainte Marie. This first change seems to have been made by the eleventh or twelfth century.

M

Secondly, the traditional name of Trémaïe for the sculptured group persisted, but to the common folk Trémaïe seemed indisputably to imply three Marys; and so the number of those who arrived in the miraculous voyage was increased so that it should provide for three women named Mary. There is some difficulty in determining just which Marys were fixed upon, as there is also uncertainty as to the precise number and identity of the various Marys spoken of in the gospels. At any rate, Mary of Bethany and Mary Magdalene are two of the three; the third is usually identified with Mary, the mother of James. Conformably with this change, the little seaport, to-day remote and insignificant, with a medieval church much larger than the present population requires, has for centuries been called by the plural name, Les Saintes Maries. There is documentary evidence that this change was effected between the tenth and fourteenth centuries.

And, in the third place, a much larger company of passengers than the original tradition could have included has now been assembled on the little barque set adrift to perish in the broad Mediterranean, but miraculously brought to shore in Provence. Some old French verses are extant, telling the story of this legendary incident. Two stanzas, literally translated without the metre or rhymes of the original, read as follows:

> Enter, Sara, this shallow boat
> With Lazarus, Martha, and Maximinus,
> Cleon, Trophimus, Saturninus,
> The three Marys and Marcellus,
> Eutropius and Martial, Sidonius and Joseph;
> In this ship you will perish.

(The speaker represents the Jewish persecutors who set the little company adrift; and Sara, of whom we shall hear more presently, was, according to the received tradition, a black Egyptian servant of the Marys.)

> Go without sail and without rigging,
> Without mast or anchor or tiller,
> Without food, without an oar;
> Go forward to dismal shipwreck;
> Withdraw yourselves from here, leave us in peace;
> Go to destruction amid the billows.*

From this augmented company, many of the cities in that part of Provence have taken their patron saints. Indeed, one motive for increasing the list of passengers may have been the desire of one city not to be outdone by a neighbouring city which already had a saint direct from Palestine. Thus Lazarus is patron saint of Marseilles; Martha, as we have seen, of Tarascon; and their respective burial places there are still shown and revered. St Trophimus became the first bishop of Arles. Mary Magdalene retired into the wild, mountainous region north of the battlefield of Aix, and the grotto is to be seen there in which she lived and died. Her relics repose at St Maximin, which is named after another of the ship's company, as St Saturnin is after still another.

---

* Entrez, Sara, dans la nacelle, Allez sans voile et sans cordage,
  Lazare, Marthe, et Maximin, Sans mât, sans ancre, sans timon,
  Cléon, Trophime, Saturnin, Sans aliments, sans aviron;
  Les trois Maries et Marcelle, Allez faire un triste naufrage!
  Eutrope et Martial, Sidoine Retirez-vous d'ici, laissez nous
           avec Joseph;   en repos;
  Vous périrez dans cette nef. Allez crever parmi des flots.

At the little seaport town of Les Saintes Maries the other two Marys remained with their servant, Sara, and their shrines, marking their place of burial, are in the great medieval church near the shore. Here, every springtime, near the end of May, worshippers and pilgrims gather to do them honour. In one of the chapels of the church are treasured certain old carved figures, about life-size, of the two Marys in their boat. On the day of the festival in memory of the landing, these figures, robed and crowned, are carried out into the sea, which is then blessed by the bishop. Even more picturesque is the gathering of gipsies to the shrine. For the gipsies of the South have adopted as their special patroness black Sara, the Egyptian servant of the Marys, and, as her fête-day comes round each spring, gipsy caravans make their way, not only from all Provence, but from far beyond, even from Spain and Italy, to the church in Les Saintes Maries. The gipsies assemble in the crypt below the body of the church (where the ceremonies of the Catholic faith are held in honour of the two Christian saints) and in this crypt they celebrate their own rites, descended, in part, from a time more ancient than the days when Christianity first came to Provence, or when Martha, the prophetess, gave counsel to Marius.

In tracing the development of the legend connected with the family of Bethany, the other story, of Marius and his victory, would seem to have dropped out of sight. Except for the connecting link of the figures of the Trémaïé, the two legends have been kept distinct in this account. But that is not done by the common people of Provence. Every man and every woman in those parts knows both the story of the famous victory and the story of the coming of the Marys with Martha and Lazarus. Not merely are both stories equally believed to be historical fact, but they are often merged in one or commingled and confused in all sorts of ways by the common folk, who have little knowledge of history and do not appreciate distinctions between quite different periods of the past. This uncritical blending of the two stories is amusingly illustrated in a passage of one of the less familiar of Scott's novels, *Anne of Geierstein*. In this story, a prominent figure is Margaret of Anjou, wife of Henry VI of England, and daughter of the famous King Réné of Provence. After the death of her husband and the downfall of the Lancastrian cause, Margaret found shelter in her native France. According to Scott (who, consciously or not, is in error on this point), it was in her early home in Provence that she took refuge, and in the novel an English Lancastrian noble comes incognito to consult with Margaret at the monastery of Sainte Victoire, where she is represented as living in retirement. "This nobleman's Provençal guide," Scott writes, "continued to expatiate on the fame of the mountain and monastery. They derived their name, he said, from a great victory gained by a Roman general named Caio Mario against two large armies of Saracens—in gratitude to Heaven for which victory Caio Mario vowed to build a monastery on the mountain for the service of the Virgin Mary, in honour of whom he had been baptized. In short," Scott continues, "he mentioned many circumstances which showed how accurately tradition will preserve the particulars of ancient events, even while forgetting, misstating, and confounding dates and persons." Scott was deeply learned in the traditional lore of his own country; how he became acquainted with this legend of Provence I have failed to discover.

The sort of confusion noted by Scott a century ago still persists. A more recent illustration is given by Mme Duclaux, a distinguished woman of letters, who, although bearing since marriage a French name, is herself of English birth. Describing a visit to Provence, she tells how, close to St Remy, near Avignon, on the site of an old Roman town, are two monuments, one an arch erected by Julius Cæsar to commemorate his defeat of the Gallic rebellion under Vercingetorix, the other a triumphal monument of peculiar grace, probably also erected by Cæsar to commemorate the double victory of his uncle, Marius, over the Teutons at Aquae Sextiae and the Cimbri at Vercellae. Carved in relief upon it are battle-scenes with barbarians, and there are also at the top, within a sort of miniature temple, two tall figures in the Roman toga. The prevailing, but not unanimous, opinion of archaeological and other experts is that these represent Marius and Catulus, his colleague in the second of the two battles. But the peasants of the neighbourhood have other explanations. Some say they are the twin emperors, Julius and Cæsar; others connect them with the local victory over the

Teutons, and explain the figures as being Caius and Marius; others, again, say they are Marius and his wife. "But," writes Mme Duclaux, "one shepherd offered me the best explanation: 'These two figures,' said he, 'represent the great Caius Marius and the prophetess Martha, the sister of Lazarus and the patroness of our Provence. They were, as you may say, a pair of friends.' 'Dear me,' said I, 'I thought there was a hundred years or so between them.' 'Maybe,' said the good man, 'that may well be, madame; but none the less they remained an excellent pair of friends.'"

In this tangled tale of Provence, then, we have, in a sense, an epitome of all legends. All the chief features that characterize the growth of legends are present: the amazing way in which the unaided memory of simple, unlettered folk will retain for centuries the events of the past, while at the same time perpetually altering and transforming this or that detail; the introduction of alien elements through confusion or misunderstanding or pure accident; the invention of episodes to explain some puzzling survival; the intrusion of the irrelevant or the haphazard, and its growth in emphasis and importance, like the young cuckoo which finally ousts the legitimate nestlings. When the memory of historical facts can be so persistently retained, and yet, at the same time, so grotesquely perverted, great caution is needed in estimating the historical value of a legend. Like so many modern newspaper stories, they are neither wholly to be trusted nor wholly to be disbelieved.

CENTRALIZATION IN EDUCATIONAL
POLICY

PREFATORY NOTE.—For the last half-century the most persistent educational problem in Ontario has been the relation between the central authority (the Department of Education) and the local authorities (the teachers and the trustees). The origin and the nature of the problem will emerge more clearly in the pages which follow. Each political party in turn, when in opposition, has criticized the government for its policy of centralized and autocratic control; but each party, when it has itself gained office, has continued that policy and, sooner or later, has increased the powers of the central Department at the expense of local autonomy and initiative.

In 1921 a large and representative committee on secondary-school education was appointed by the Farmers' Group government of the day, and, after long consideration, presented a report, in which proposals were made that seemed to promise an enlargement of the liberty of action of the local authorities. It was on that occasion, before a large gathering of secondary-school principals and assistants from the whole province, that the following address was given. It does not discuss the details of the proposals then just made public, but deals rather with the fundamental principles involved in the whole question of centralized educational policy, and such value as it has is, therefore, independent of the particular time and circumstances of its delivery.

As regards centralization in education, Ontario almost of necessity stands in a quite different position from either England or the United States. England has virtually no national constitution except usage, descended from the past and modified from time to time as need arises. Side by side with this unwritten constitution exists an incredible number of local and municipal rights and institutions, of equal or even greater antiquity and of equally uncontested validity. Any serious attempt to co-ordinate and supervise the local educational institutions belongs to quite recent history, and centralized authority has great difficulty in making headway against the inherited tradition of local freedom.

In the United States which, on the other hand, has a rigid written constitution, education is left to the jurisdiction of the individual states. These also have their written constitutions, and within each state a uniform centralized system of education might easily have been set up, especially in the newer states. Yet as a matter of fact this has not been done. Whether it is because of the example of the oldest states, which had well-developed local institutions before the time came for a written state constitution, or whether it is because of the general diffusion of an enthusiastic attachment to liberty, at any rate in the United States also an unbroken tradition of local autonomy in education has grown up throughout the entire nation.

In Ontario very little had been done in pioneer days to establish any local institutions before the authority of the State stepped in, not at first to regulate and supervise the few existing schools, but to provide educational facilities that were almost wholly lacking. And thus, both in theory (because of our constitution) and in practice (because of the conditions under which this province grew up), education has always with us been organized under a central authority, and any powers that the local authorities or the individual community may possess are derived from this central authority, and not from any traditional usage or any recognized inherent right. Furthermore, the educational system of the province has been built up almost wholly under the regime of three men of strong convictions and forceful wills—Ryerson, Ross, and Seath —under whom the inevitable tendency was towards greater centralization and ever increasing regulation from above.

Between the two extremes of excessive centralization and utter lack of co-ordination there must surely be some golden mean, at which each country should aim. If England is to attain this, it will be, no doubt, by increased co-ordination and more supervision by the State. If Ontario is to attain it, the movement must be in precisely the opposite direction, by increasing the freedom of local authorities, by decentralization and devolution. But even if it be agreed that the general direction of the movement has been correctly stated, the precise distance that must be traversed to reach the mean will not be easy to determine. The right decision can be reached only by trial and testing, and the final verdict must be pronounced by experience, not by theory. There still, however, remains some room for reasoning and discussion, based on the experience of the past and guided by general principles of recognized value.

For each of the rival tendencies good arguments can be adduced. Each has certain advantages, and each has also certain disadvantages. Without elaborating these, it will be sufficient to indicate very briefly what can be said for and against the policy of centralization in educational affairs. For centralization, the great arguments are that increased efficiency is attained and that the schools are delivered from the mistakes of inexperience and unwise enthusiasm; all the arguments, in short, that can be urged for an enlightened and benevolent despotism ruling over those who are incompetent to direct their own course and so are apt to go astray. Against centralization are urged its tendency to rigid uniformity and mass production, its lack of adaptability to varying local conditions, and, above all, its destruction of initiative, resulting in apathy of interest and atrophy of power; all the arguments, in short, that can be urged in support of a democratic form of government among a free people, in which experience and free discussion must be relied upon to eliminate error and to secure ultimate efficiency along with a fully developed individuality.

In fact, the two antagonistic policies are essentially the ideal of German *Kultur* and the ideal of western democracy; and the issue between them was fought out in the recent war. If the lessons of that war and our own experience of the working of a centralized educational system in Ontario have not shown in which direction it is advisable for us to move, a short address like this will scarcely suffice to settle the question. Instead of arguing the point, I shall assume that a reasonable freedom, with its accompaniment of local or individual responsibility, is necessary for the development of the finest qualities of personality and for the production of the best fruits of our western civilization; and, assuming this, I proceed to consider what should be the nature and limits of the activity of the central educational authority, and what, therefore, should be the nature and extent of the decentralization we should desire to see brought about in our system of education.

The first and the great problem is to decide where to draw the line between what the State should control and what should be the province of the local authority. It may help us to solve this problem if we begin by asking: What is the special concern and interest of the State in educational affairs? What, ultimately, is it that justifies the State's exercise of authority in this sphere? Whether this takes the form of pressure or of restraint, of compulsion or of prohibition, makes no difference; and, what is more often forgotten, there is no real distinction between the State's acting directly itself, and the State's requiring others, such as a local board of trustees or a school principal, to act. What a local authority does by direction of the State is not its own free action, but the State's.

At this point of our inquiry we may profitably avail ourselves of a formula which was widely, if not universally, accepted in England a few years ago, and which played a great part in the discussions leading up to the passage of the Fisher Bill in Great Britain.

With the approval of practically every important class or group of people in that country, we may assume that the interest of the State is to "secure for all classes the training in character and intelligence which befits the citizens of a free and civilized nation." Let us see whether this formula will help us, and how far it will take us, in defining the sphere of action of the central authority.

In the first place, this principle involves compulsory education and the enforcement thereof by such means as are in practice found most effective. If all classes ought to receive the training in character and intelligence which befits the citizens of a free and civilized nation, then the State cannot afford to allow either local apathy, or parental greed, indifference, or short-sightedness, to interfere with what is so vital to the best interests both of the State or community as a whole and of the individual child itself.

Secondly, this principle, if followed out, involves the obligation on the part of the State to see that children are enabled to profit by the public provision made for their education. There is great wastage because of the degree to which ill health (due to improper physical conditions and to neglect of preventive or remedial measures) interferes with the training of the child to become an effective member of the community. The need (real or alleged) to leave school early in order to earn wages is another cause of wastage; and a third is the mixture of defective with normal children. All these are matters which the State in its own interest cannot afford to neglect as it has neglected them. In pursuance of this policy the State may have to exercise oversight of health, to regulate sanitary conditions, to make provision for physical training, to enforce adolescent attendance acts, and even, in case of necessity under our imperfect economic system, to give State aid to needy and hungry children, and, finally, it may have to make special grants to embarrassed or backward communities within its borders.

The War years revealed to England something that social reformers had long been preaching to deaf ears: that a terrible mistake was being made in neglecting the conditions under which so many thousands of children were growing up. In the face of a declining birth-rate and the losses caused by the War, it would be nothing short of criminal if in the next generation as large a proportion of England's youth should be found to be physically unfit as the recruiting depots then discovered. If conditions in Ontario are not as bad as they were in England, they are still too bad to be allowed to exist any longer. The State may act through school boards or through boards of health or through the two in combination; but whatever agency be used, it is the duty and the interest of the State, in all its schemes of educational reform, to keep in view the physical, as well as the mental health and development of the school population. This question of the supervision of the physical health of pupils should not be confused with the question of military drill for school children. The latter may be more spectacular and may appear to many to be more patriotic; the former is of infinitely greater importance. For if the nation can see to it that both the bodies and the minds of our growing youth shall be well nurtured and well developed by the most enlightened methods, so as to be alert and sound and vigorous, then the nation will be sure to have the best possible material both for the normal activities of the citizen in time of peace and for the extraordinary duties he may be called on to perform in time of war. The experience of this recent war proves that, for a citizen army with Anglo-Saxon ideals and traditions, a sound body and a sound mind and character are far more essential than long preliminary training in the minutiae of the soldier's drill.

Thirdly, it follows from the principle we have assumed that it is the province of the State to see that an adequate supply of properly trained teachers is available. And this will not stop with the provision of training schools, the holding of examination tests, and the supervision of conditions of employment. The State should also endeavour to make the profession of teaching reasonably attractive. Such matters as permanence of tenure, social status and influence in the community, teachers' residences—all these are things in which the State, as well as the community, has its part to play. And, fourthly and finally, there is abundant room for the State's activity in educational propaganda, in the awakening of public interest, in the spreading of information, and in the encouragement of progressive measures and local experiments.

So far, our argument would seem to have enlarged the sphere of the State's activities rather than to have restricted it. This would be in harmony with the general tendency observable in all civilized countries in recent decades to widen the sphere of governmental activity. The growing sense of the intimate connection between the welfare of the community and the welfare of the individual has tended to make all government, both national and local, more paternal than it used to be. But wise paternal government is not incompatible with reasonable self-government, as every sensible parent knows. It will, moreover, be observed that most of the various forms of activity that we have been considering involve the most intimate co-operation and consultation between the central and the local authorities, and depend for their success quite as much upon the development of initiative and resourcefulness in the latter as upon wise forethought and guidance in the former.

None the less, if our analysis were to end here, the total effect could scarcely be called decentralization; at best it would be centralization tempered by co-operation. But, in fact, nothing has been said as yet of a large sphere of action in which the Ontario Department of Education busily occupies itself. A conviction has long been held by many that the Department has in the past been too exclusively concerned, not with the activities we have found legitimately belonging to it, but with the regulation of other matters which often might better have been left largely to local control. Too much of its energy

has been directed, partly to making minute and detailed regulations to be uniformly applied in the
organization and conduct of the schools, and partly
to building up a system of inspection that would
ensure the observance of these regulations and pre-
scriptions. Zeal for progress has always been present,
no doubt; but too often it has merely taken the form
of so amending existing regulations as to substitute
one uniform set of rules, imposed from above, for
another. There would be more real progress if the
State were to withdraw from many fields in which it
has been exercising almost despotic powers, and, in
return, were to assume other and more proper func-
tions that hitherto have been discharged in an inadequate and haphazard fashion. A harsher critic might
say that the Department of Education has been tithing
mint and cummin, while neglecting the weightier matters of the law; that it has left undone things which it
ought to have done, and has busied itself overmuch
with things which it ought to have left to others to do.

For when we come to such things as school organization, prescription of courses of study, provision of
text-books, and methods of teaching, and ask what is
the State's peculiar concern in the detailed regulation
of such matters, the principle which has so far been
our guide now seems to fail us, the principle that the
State should seek to secure for all classes the training
in character and intelligence which befits the citizens
of a free and civilized nation. Except perhaps in
a few minor details, it is difficult to see any larger
interest of the whole province which would justify

N

interference with considerable local freedom in these matters. No one would seriously contend that the end in view (the character and intelligence befitting a free citizen) can be attained in but one way, all other ways being wrong or inferior, and that therefore this one right way should be so carefully marked out that even wayfaring men, though teachers, shall not err therein, but shall have definite directions given them what subjects are to be taken up at each stage, and in what order, and how much shall be studied weekly and how often and for how long and by what methods and out of what books.

The advocates of centralized control over such matters freely admit that, of course, many trustee boards, many schools, many teachers (perhaps even a majority) do not require this careful guidance and supervision; but they contend that there is much inexperience and much unwisdom abroad in the land, and that there are places where intervention is necessary to save the pupils from the blunders and folly of their teachers or the trustees. Hence, it is argued, to prevent muddle-headedness here and negligence there, definite rules are required; and these, of course, must be made uniform and applicable to all, on the principle of democratic equality; as if, forsooth, because India long needed to be kept in leading-strings, Canada and Australia also should have been denied self-government. There may, admittedly, be localities or teachers unfit to be trusted with much freedom; but even these should be given all the freedom with which they can be trusted (and perhaps a little more), that so they may learn gradually to use still more freedom. Instead of this, the practice here criticized would, because of a few, keep all under tutelage, and so would eventually render all unfit for freedom and incapable of self-government. The State is not abdicating its proper function of guidance, advice, and oversight, nor evading its ultimate responsibility, when it allows a large measure of reasonable freedom. As in the training of our sons, that may be the best way of producing the strong and self-reliant character all agree is desirable.

In the pupil's earlier years, in the primary grades, it may be that the training of all our future citizens should follow very similar lines, though even here it should never be forgotten that the teacher is not dealing with inanimate material where machine-like regularity and rigid uniformity may be unobjectionable, or even, for mass production, highly desirable. The development of the young belongs in the region of the spirit, whose movements can be subjected to an inflexible regimen only with deplorable results. Moreover, the teacher, too, has an individuality that should have room in which to display itself. Teachers, good teachers, differ greatly, both in the methods by which, and in the subjects through which, they are able to arouse interest and stimulate the growth of intelligence in the plastic minds of young children. Our high-school teachers have often cause to deplore the fact that so many pupils come to them from the primary schools with all desire to learn gone, with all the keen interest they once had in new knowledge somehow killed. If a teacher of young children in the elementary school has the gift some- how, anyhow, of keeping alive and alert the child's native curiosity and its interest in discovering new truth, we should hesitate to be too meticulous about inquiring whether there has also been imparted a minutely defined quantum of the formal curriculum.

But however uniform may be the earlier training, certainly by the time the secondary school has been reached, well-defined lines of cleavage begin to appear, and individual tastes, aptitudes, and powers begin to assert themselves. When this stage is reached, only an omniscient department of education could advise and prescribe as wisely as can the teacher who knows the pupil as an individual. Hence it is eminently proper that just here should be the point in school organization where the report just laid before you proposes to make a break in the custom of long years, and to give to the principal and his staff new powers and new responsibilities. The report, moreover, recognizes that, besides the two classes of pupils (the prospective teacher and the prospective university student) whose courses of study are at least in some particulars necessarily fixed, there is a much larger number of those whom our school should be prepar- ing for their future life in the community as men and women and citizens, and whose legitimate needs, hitherto so poorly provided for, can be adequately supplied only by giving much greater freedom to the local authorities than they now enjoy.

To the proposals laid before you I can foresee two

objections. Some will think that this report does not go far enough in advising the granting of more freedom, and that the degree to which decentralization is involved is slight in comparison with what an ideal condition of things would bring about. I quite agree that this should be regarded only as the first step. But in learning to walk, after being in leading-strings so long, it is well at first to go cautiously. The whole cause of freedom would be imperilled by "rash haste, half-sister to delay." By using the new powers wisely we shall best prove ourselves worthy of greater freedom, and those who doubt the wisdom of even this first step will be most effectually silenced. We have been living in a walled enclosure whose grounds are most scrupulously kept, with well-marked paths and carefully paved walks, while plenty of signs announce: Keep to the walks; Do not pluck the flowers; No thoroughfare. And now a door has been opened leading into open country where there are no such well-ordered ways and where the footing is not so secure. We had better, at first, not wander too far, or extend our range so heedlessly as to get lost, even if we do catch glimpses of most alluring prospects some distance farther on.

A second possible objection is from the opposite quarter; that too much responsibility is being thrown on the teacher. This reluctance to assume responsibility is itself one of the results of the long-continued policy of centralized regulation, and one of the chief grounds for condemning or deploring that policy. "The more thoroughly," it has been said, "a man's life is ordered for him, the less capable does he become of ordering it for himself." He loses the power of initiative; the will to choose and decide becomes atrophied; and when he must choose, sound judgment is lacking. One of the most interesting of the War books was a survey of German ideals and character, entitled *The Nemesis of Docility*, by Edmond Holmes. The title suggests the line of thought developed by him, that "the tendency of pressure emanating from an autocratic State is to crush individuality and all that individuality implies—initiative, self-reliance, independence of thought, responsibility to conscience, force of character—predisposes one, in other words, to substitute responsibility to external authority for responsibility to his own inward light." Another and better-known writer, the veteran educationist, Michael Sadler, in a penetrating analysis of German educational methods, wrote as follows: "From our experience of German education we may draw lessons for the guidance of our educational policy. If we are prudent we shall avoid an excess of bureaucratic control. We shall frankly recognize the value of official experience, and of the guidance and prestige which the resources of government enable it to give to educational effort. But we shall guard ourselves against setting too much store by administrative tidiness in our educational system. We shall remind ourselves that, in the difficult days of social readjustment which will follow the war, there will be more need than ever for variety of experiment, for variety of educational tradition, for variety of responsible initiative. The most valuable things in our education depend on encouragement being given to each school to have a personality of its own. But to have a personality, a school must have (so far as a reasonable degree of public order allows) freedom of growth and self-direction in its purpose." The Englishman is writing of a freedom which he already possesses and which he prizes supremely. For us, such freedom has been hitherto an aspiration, an ideal which now at long last our good fortune seems to be placing within our grasp. "Freedom of growth and self-direction, so far as a reasonable degree of public order allows"—we ask for no more; we should be satisfied with nothing less. That which the English writer emphasizes is one (perhaps the greatest) gain to be looked for in the new vista opening before us—the greater opportunity for the development of initiative and self-reliance, for the production of personality in the school, in the teacher, and in the pupil, the future citizen.

And a second gain which should come from giving increased powers to local authorities is the new interest that would be aroused in the community. The great objection to democracy and self-government—the objection of Socrates and Plato, of Matthew Arnold and Carlyle—has always been that the people at large are not competent. The best answer I have seen to this ancient objection is Montesquieu's restatement of Aristotle's argument: that it is not to be expected that they should be competent, nor does it much matter; the main thing is that they should be interested. To replace apathy and indifference by interest—how many educational problems this would solve! A new life might begin to spring up in a community where parents and trustees and teachers could discuss the local problems of education (not the mere provision or repair of a building or the hiring of a janitor, but the things that touch the deepest welfare of their own children) and might have some reasonable expectation of their discussions actually bearing fruit in speedy action. This would be one of the surest ways to put the school and the teacher in their rightful place in the community, and it would go farther than anything I can imagine to reconcile the tax-payer to adequate expenditure on education.

SUPPLEMENTARY NOTE.—The outcome was disappointing. The government which appointed the committee soon went out of office, and no such reform as was looked for came to pass. The Department of Education did not make the expected provision for increased freedom of action or do anything to lessen the pressure of bureaucratic control; and, more disheartening still, it became evident that a new generation of teachers had grown up, so accustomed to being guided at all points by the Department's direction and supervision, that they showed few signs of welcoming, and still fewer of demanding, larger powers and more liberty. The Nemesis of Docility had overtaken them, and a condition of things in reality worse in many ways than that which their predecessors had chafed under and thought intolerable is now quietly accepted by them as part of the established order of the universe.

That conditions have not improved since this address was first written would seem to be borne out by the following evidence:

(1) From the official report * made in 1927 to the English Board of Education by His Majesty's Inspector E. G. Savage after six months' observation of the Ontario secondary schools. In this frank and comprehensive survey many things are commended and many others are criticized. In particular, the inspector, with his English background, has only disapproval for the complete centralization which he found in Ontario, involving, as it did, the minute regulation of almost every phase of school life, with little or nothing left to the initiative of principals and teachers, however capable of creative work, and resulting, so he observed, in their general acquiescence in being but cogs in a machine.

(2) From the address given in 1936 by the President of the Canadian Education Association, Dr G. F. Rogers, Chief Inspector of Secondary Schools of Ontario:

"Personally, I am strongly opposed to bureaucratic administration of educational institutions. The trouble in my own province is that for some reason or other teachers are not keen to exercise the freedom that they have."

* This valuable and too little-known report, entitled *Secondary Education in Ontario*, is Educational Pamphlet No. 53, published by His Majesty's Stationery Office, London, England.

DEMOSTHENES AND THE GERMAN EMPEROR

A MODERN PHILIPPIC

PREFATORY NOTE.—Repeatedly, in his public addresses, Demosthenes strove to awaken the Athenians to a realization of their danger from Philip of Macedon's unscrupulous aggressiveness, and, while there was yet time, to arouse them to resolute action against him. In 1916, when the United States, in spite of German ruthlessness, seemed content with its policy of neutrality and had just re-elected President Wilson because "he kept us out of the war," the parallel between the ancient situation and the modern was sufficiently striking to suggest the following experiment. Out of seven different speeches of Demosthenes, passages of varying length were selected and so interwoven as to make one connected speech that, with obvious substitutions of proper names, might be imagined to have been addressed by some indignant citizen of the United States to his lethargic countrymen. The verbal alterations necessary for this purpose proved to be singularly few; at least ninety-five per cent of the following mosaic is unchanged and unadapted Demosthenes. Apart from the modern application, this composite "Philippic" may serve to give a reader unfamiliar with Demosthenes some not wholly inadequate conception of his outspoken and forceful eloquence. The German Emperor, of course, long ago ceased to be either a hero to his own people or a bogy to other nations; but he may still be regarded as personifying a dangerous and evil spirit which the growth of Hitlerism and Nazism to-day shows to have been scotched, not killed, in 1918. Nor, as a warning againſt the dangers to the United States of a policy of isolation and indifference, have the arguments of Demoſthenes even yet quite loſt all their point.

The English translations of the passages used are, by the kind permission of the Clarendon Press, Oxford, taken from the admirable version of *The Public Orations of Demoſthenes*, by A. W. Pickard-Cambridge.

If ever the moſt anxious deliberation was required, it is in the present crisis, fellow-citizens; but my greateſt difficulty is not to know *what* advice to give you, but rather to know in what words to frame that advice. For I am convinced that for the moſt part the objects of our policy have slipped from our grasp, not because we do not underſtand what our duty is, but because we will not do it. If you are in the mood to liſten to nothing but what will gratify your pride, at a time when you ſtand in the graveſt peril, I have nothing to say; but if you are willing to liſten while I tell you, without flattery, reserve, or evasion, what your intereſts and your honour require, I am prepared to speak.

The present crisis seems almoſt to cry aloud that you muſt take matters into your own hands yonder, that you muſt act decisively, and not fall into the same error you have so often recently made. For in all our diplomatic interchanges with regard to the acts of violence by which Philip contravenes the peace, I observe that, although the ſtatements on our side are always manifeſtly juſt and humane, yet practically nothing is accomplished that would make it worth while to have sent these remonſtrances.

I wish you to realize these two points: firſt, the unprofitableness of perpetually sacrificing your intereſts; and second, the reſtless activity which is a part of Philip's very being. For if it is his fixed resolve that he muſt always be aiming at something greater than he has yet attained, and our fixed resolve that we will never set ourselves resolutely to do our duty—what can you expect to be the end of the matter? I am amazed that any one who views the paſt policy and actions of Philip can be free from alarm, or can imagine that they involve no peril to this nation. What use, I ask you, has he always made of his power? He has viewed everything in the light of his own ambition and desire for universal conqueſt; he has taken no thought for peace or tranquillity or juſtice; he sees that you would reprobate the infamy of his policy, but he believes that you also would shrink from acting againſt him or doing anything effective. He is intoxicated with the greatness of his success and entertains many a vision of world dominion. Does he not write expressly: "I am at peace with those who choose to obey me"? But we remain isolated; we enter into no combination for mutual support and friendship; we look on while the man becomes greater; and, while our neighbours are being ruined, every one is so eager for profit that no one cares for the safety of civilization.

I say nothing of the Thracian cities annihilated by him with such savagery that a visitor to the spot would find it difficult to tell that they had ever been inhabited; I am silent in regard to the extirpation of the great

Phocian race; I speak not of the condition of Thessaly, where he has robbed the cities of their governments, and enslaved them not by whole cities but by whole tribes at a time. But I ask you, is he not also *our* enemy? Has he not levied war on the property and the lives of our citizens? Is he not a barbarian? Is he not anything that you may choose to call him? Mark the situation, men of Athens; mark the pitch to which the man's outrageous insolence has reached, when he does not even give you a choice between action and inaction, but his agents plot against you in your own land, and his representatives use threatening and haughty language to you. He is not the man to rest content with his present conquests; he is always casting his net wider, and while we procrastinate and sit idle, he is setting his toils around us on every side.

In God's name, is there one of you so innocent as not to know that, if we pay no heed, the war will be transferred from Olynthus to our own country? You have to choose, not between war and peace, but between intervening now in the war yonder or having him make war in his own time on you here. If the resistance to him in Olynthus is maintained, you may remain secure in the enjoyment of your land; but if Philip conquers there, who is to hinder him from attacking us? "But, my good sir," you say, "he will not want to attack us." Yet would it not be the strangest thing if, when he has the power, he does not carry out the policy that he has clearly been planning from the first, and execute the threats which from

time to time escape him? His design is steadily
moving towards fulfilment; and, though I shrink from
precise conjecture, I fear its accomplishment may even
now be only too close at hand. Heaven grant that
the time may not come when the truth of my words
will be tested with all severity! Yet we sit idle, and
the time when we should be acting we spend on debating; but events will not wait for our slothful
evasion of our duty. If we do not help ourselves,
we cannot expect any friends to help us, much less the
gods. It is no wonder that Philip, who is himself a
man of action and always keenly alert, who lets no
opportunity go, no occasion pass, should get the better
of us who delay action and content ourselves with
diplomatic notes and requests for fuller information.

No official message is worth anything unless we are
willing resolutely to follow it up with action. If
messages by themselves would realize their objects
unaided, Philip would have paid the penalty long ago.
But it is not so, men of Athens. It is by deeds and
actions, not by words, that a policy of encroachment
must be arrested; and yet those who direct your policy
will not face the duty of proposing action, for fear of
unpopularity with you, though they recognize the
atrocity of Philip's acts; and you yourselves, though
you use the language of justice and humanity, and
appreciate it from the lips of others, are nevertheless
absolutely inert, when it is a question of preventing
him from executing the designs in which he is engaged.
The inevitable consequence is that each excels in that
to which he gives time and thought: Philip in deeds,

you in words. If it is enough for you that your
words are more juSt than his, your course is easy
and no labour is involved in it; but if the evil of the
present situation is to be corre&ed, if its advance is
not to continue, unperceived, until we are confronted
with a power so great that we cannot even raise a
hand in our own defence, then we muSt mend our
ways, and we muSt prefer the counsels that can save
us to those which are easy and attra&ive.

See to it then, men of Athens, that your representatives may not only have fine words to speak, but
firm a&ions of yours to point to. Let it be seen that
we are already in a&ion in a manner worthy of Athens.
Words without deeds muSt always appear a vain and
empty thing; and above all when they come from our
Chief MagiStrate. For the more he seems to excel in
the fluent use of such language, the less are his words
heeded by any one. And when you send forth merely
empty notes and pious hopes from your government,
you achieve nothing that you ought to achieve; your
enemies laugh at you, and your friends hang their
heads in shame.

Surely, men of Athens, it is one of the gods—one
that blushes for our ina&ion—that has inspired Philip
with his reStless aggressiveness. If he were content
to remain at peace with us, in possession of what he
has already won by conqueSt or by false dealing—if
he had no ulterior designs—even then the record
againSt us as a people would be a record of shame
and cowardice and dishonour. But as he is always
grasping after something more, it may be that his

conduct will bring you into the field, unless your spirit has utterly departed.

If indeed some god were to offer us his guarantee (for no human guarantee would be sufficient in so grave a matter) that, if we remain quiet and let everything pass, Philip will not in the end come and attack ourselves, then—although before God and every Heavenly Power it would be unworthy of you and of your forefathers to abandon all the rest of civilization to slavery for the sake of your own ease; although for my part I would rather have died than have suggested such a thing—yet if another proposes it and can convince you, let it be so; take no action; let everything go. But if no such guarantee is possible, if it is clear that the wider the mastery we allow him to gain, the more difficult and powerful a foe we shall have to deal with, what further subterfuge is open to us? Why do we delay? When shall we ever be willing to do our duty? What are we waiting for? "We are waiting," you say, "till it is necessary to act." But surely the strongest necessity that a free people can experience is the shame which they must feel at their position. However, the hour of compulsion, as free men judge it, is not only here already, but has long passed; and we must now pray that the compulsion that belongs to slaves may not come upon us.

With this knowledge, men of Athens, I say that now, if ever, you must make your resolve, rouse all your energies, and give your minds to this war. There is no longer any reason or excuse remaining which can justify you in refusing to do your duty;

you must get rid of all excuses and all deficiencies. That is the policy for a nation with a reputation such as yours; but if you fancy that some other people will save civilization, while you run away from the task, you are mistaken. The task is yours; it is the prerogative that your forefathers won and through many a great peril bequeathed to you. And though all but ourselves should give way and become slaves, we at least must battle for freedom.

It is not so long since you returned from your expedition in aid of the Euboeans,* when you went forth in defence of the rights of others and, without thought of your opportunities for gain, sought only to secure for others their just rights, and spent freely your wealth and bravely bore the brunt of the dangers of the campaign. I am amazed that you now submit lightheartedly to the reproach which must follow any short-comings in the struggle for human rights and liberty. I am amazed that you now shrink from warfare and hesitate to make any sacrifice even to secure your own safety; that you who seized your weapons and marched forth to resist Corinthians or Megareans, now are sitting idle, allowing Philip to enslave Hellenic cities and not realizing that both your own honour and your own existence are at stake.

When the envoys from Amphipolis † came and urged us to intervene on behalf of their outraged people, had we continued to display the eagerness we once displayed in the deliverance of the Euboeans, we

* *Sc.*, The Cubans, in the war with Spain.
† *Sc.*, Belgium.

o

should have been free from all the trouble that we have had since. And again, when news kept coming of the investment of Pydna,* Potidaea, Methone, Pagasae, and all the rest—I will not stay to enumerate them all —if we had acted at once, with the energy we ought to have shown, we should now have found Philip much less arrogant and difficult to deal with. As it is, we are always sacrificing the present occasion, always fancying that the future will turn out well of itself, and so we have suffered Philip to attain his present dangerous power.

And there are actually some among us who are trying to bring about the very thing that Philip would pray Heaven for. Whenever any question of our relations with Philip arises, at once someone comes forward and talks of the blessings of peace, or the difficulty of maintaining a large force, and of designs on the part of certain persons to plunder our funds; with other talk of the same kind, which enables them to delay your action and gives Philip time to do what he wishes unopposed. Now, if it is possible for us to remain honourably at peace, I agree we ought to do so; but if another, with weapons in his hands, holds out to you the name of peace, while his acts are the acts of war, what course remains open to us but that of resistance? Is there a man in his senses who would judge by words and not by facts whether another's attitude is one of peace or war? There is no need to persuade *you* to keep the peace; it is the man who is committing acts of war that we

* *Sc.*, The sinking of the *Lusitania, Hesperian, Arabic*, etc.

need to persuade; if *he* is persuaded, *we* are ready enough. But if any man's conception of peace is that it is a state in which Philip can master all others till at last he comes to attack ourselves, such a conception is madness. And it is moreover, mark you, a peace which you are to observe towards Philip, while he does not observe it towards you. And this it is—this power to carry on war against you without being met by any hostilities on your part—that Philip is purchasing with all the money that he is spending here.

You must come to execrate those who address you in his interest, remembering that it is impossible to master the enemies without, until you suppress those who are serving them in our midst. Yet you have reached such a pitch of folly and infatuation that you freely allow men to speak among you who are hirelings of Philip—and some of them would not even deny it—and you listen patiently to their treasonable sophistry and their arrogant abuse. And when there are those in your midst who lie to you lightheartedly about all that Philip is planning and doing, and when it is on the strength of these lying tales and assurances that you determine your policy, what must you expect?

But if we dismiss all such talk, and attend only to the certainty that the man is our enemy—that he is robbing us of our rights—that he has insulted us for a long time—that the future is in our own hands— that if we will not fight him in his country we shall perhaps be obliged to do so in our own—if we are assured of this, we shall have made up our minds aright, and shall be quit of idle words. You have not to speculate what the future will be; you have only to be assured that the future will be evil, unless you give heed and do your duty. If any of you is putting off the time of decision, he muſt surely be desirous of seeing the horrors of war close at hand, when he need only hear of them at a diſtance, and of having to seek aid for himself while now he can give aid to others. I need not point out how vaſt is the difference between war here and war in Philip's country. A few days' war on our soil would entail loss vaſtly greater than the whole expenditure necessary to avert war from this land; and besides the loss if war ever comes to our doors, there is the man's insolence, and the shame of our position, which to right-minded men is as serious as any financial loss.

The firſt essential point, therefore, is this—that you regard him as the irreconcilable foe of liberty and democracy. The very titles he bears are utterly alien to freedom. There is one great safeguard a democracy has againſt a despot, and that is—diſtruſt. For an absolute monarch is always the foe of freedom and the enemy of law, and it is never safe for a free people to be over-friendly with a tyrant. And, secondly, you muſt realize clearly that all the plans which he has been so busily contriving are, ultimately, direﬆed againſt this country, and that wherever any one is resiſting him, he is resiſting him on our behalf.

Do not imagine that his empire is built to laſt for ever, as if he were a god. He has those who hate and fear him and envy him, even among those who now

seem to be his staunchest supporters. Neither are his
affairs at present in such good order or in so satisfactory a state as might appear to a casual observer;
nor would he ever have commenced this present war,
if he had thought that he would really have to fight
as he has. He hoped at first that by his mere advance
he would carry all before him, and he has since discovered his mistake. If any of you also imagines
that Philip will maintain his hold by force, because he
has already occupied fortified posts and harbours and
similar positions, he is mistaken. It is impossible,
men of Athens, utterly impossible to acquire power
that will last by unrighteousness, by perjury, and by
falsehood. Such power holds out but for a brief
hour; it blossoms brightly with fair hopes, but time
detects the fraud, and the flower falls withered about
its stalk. As, in a house or ship, it is the foundations
that must be strongest, so, no less, must the principles
which are the foundations of men's actions be those of
truth and righteousness—qualities that are not to be
found in Philip's policy. At present all these facts
are overshadowed by his apparent prosperity. Success has a wonderful power of throwing a veil over
shameful things; but I believe that the revelation is
not far off, if Heaven be willing and you be resolute.

You must, then, keep him at the greatest possible
distance, both by diplomatic measures and by military
preparation; you must prevent him from extending
his unrighteous power, or you will have to grapple
with him at close quarters in a struggle to the death.
So long as the vessel is safe, so long must the sailor

and the captain—every man in his place—exert himself that no one may capsize it, by design or by accident; for when once the seas have overwhelmed it, all
their efforts are in vain.   So it is with us.   While we
are still safe, with our great nation, our vast resources,
our noble name, we must make preparation for resistance, with ships, with money, and with men.

And above all, men of Athens, you must be on your
guard lest, in striving to avoid war, you find yourselves
slaves.

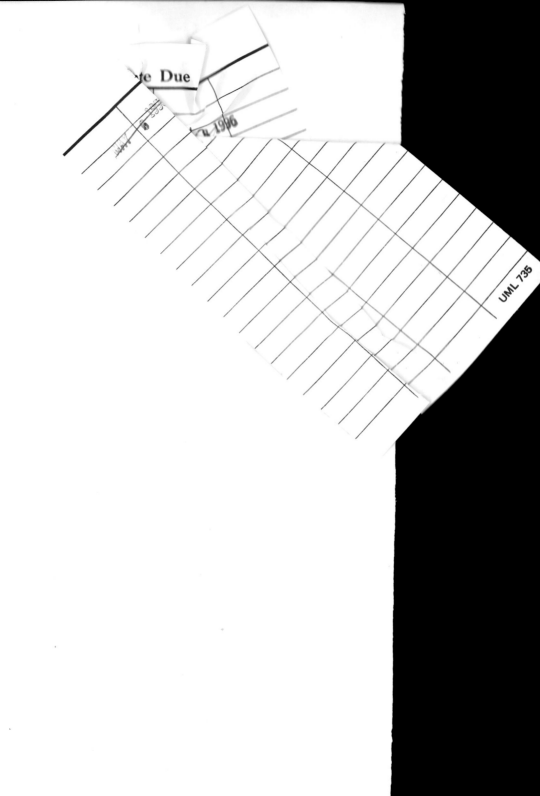